THE

AMERICANO

DREAM

THE
AMERICANO
DREAM

*How Latinos Can Achieve Success
in Business and in Life*

LIONEL SOSA

A DUTTON BOOK

DUTTON
Published by the Penguin Group
Penguin Putnam Inc., 375 Hudson Street,
New York, New York 10014, U.S.A.
Penguin Books Ltd, 27 Wrights Lane,
London W8 5TZ, England
Penguin Books Australia Ltd, Ringwood,
Victoria, Australia
Penguin Books Canada Ltd, 10 Alcorn Avenue,
Toronto, Ontario, Canada M4V 3B2
Penguin Books (N.Z.) Ltd, 182–190 Wairau Road,
Auckland 10, New Zealand

Penguin Books Ltd, Registered Offices:
Harmondsworth, Middlesex, England

First published by Dutton, an imprint of Dutton Signet,
a member of Penguin Putnam Inc.

First Printing, March, 1998
10   9   8   7   6   5   4   3   2   1

REGISTERED TRADEMARK—MARCA REGISTRADA

LIBRARY OF CONGRESS CATALOGING-IN-PUBLICATION DATA:
Sosa, Lionel.
    The Americano Dream: how Latinos can achieve success in business and in life /
Lionel Sosa.
        p.   cm.
    ISBN 0-525-94309-9
    1. Success in business—United States.   2. Hispanic American businesspeople.
3. Hispanic American business enterprises—Management.   I. Title.
    HF5386.S744   1998
    650.1'089'68073—dc21   97-28713
                                                                                          CIP

Printed in the United States of America
Set in New Baskerville
Designed by Leonard Telesca

This book is printed on acid-free paper. ∞

To my wife, Kathy
who more than anyone
has helped me be
the best person
I can be

To Mom & Dad
who always believed
I'd achieve
the Americano Dream

ACKNOWLEDGMENTS

I've had a lot of help in writing this book. The greatest help came from Richard Marek, the consummate professional who took my thoughts and put them into words that sound like a more intelligent version of myself. This book would never have seen the light of day without Richard. To you—*un millón de gracias.*

Also, *mil gracias* to Madeleine Morel and Barbara Lowenstein, the two feisty literary agents who insisted this book be written because it would have an audience. They never gave up and made sure I didn't, no matter how many rewrites it took.

Thanks to my researcher, Teresa Niño, who was invaluable in gathering facts, setting up interviews, and who shared her valuable insights and opinions.

Gracias también to all my friends and business partners—past and present—whose success stories illustrate the Latino opportunity and whose names you will find throughout this book. A special thanks to my dear friends Father Virgil Elizondo, Dr. Lou Agnese, my brother Robert Sosa, and John Phillip Santos, whose wonderful understanding of culture and history provided the foundation to build this book upon.

Thanks to my family—especially my wonderful children, Anna, Rebecca, Blanca, James, Cristina, and Vincent, as well as my two terrific stepsons, Mark and John, who read and reread more rough drafts of this than they cared to. Also to Barbie Hernandez and her friends who set up and participated in my focus groups, and to Romelia Escamilla and Jose and Shirley Martinez for their on-target suggestions.

And finally, thanks to all the patient crew at KJS, especially my wife and partner, Kathy, who accepted my frequent "disappearances" from my job while I was writing this.

Contents

INTRODUCTION

"Lionel," my mother said when I was six, "you're going to make it. Even though you're Mexican, you're going to succeed."

It was almost a mantra with her, and she repeated it often over the years—she was a determined woman, focusing always on being upwardly mobile, wanting only the best for my father and herself, and for her four children.

But to me her words were confusing. Did she mean I was going to succeed *despite* rather than *because of* who I was? That being Mexican was something to overcome, a handicap, such as dyslexia? Would I have to work harder because I *was* inferior, or would I have to do more because people would *assume* I was inferior? These mixed signals came from many people I later knew. If you were only Anglo, they seemed to say, success was a done deal. But I'd have to work harder, think harder, compete harder just to keep up. And all because—*only* because—I was Latino.

Latinos in the United States have a long and noble history.

- Our ancestors were the first immigrant group in America, the land of immigrants. We were here 125 years before the Pilgrims landed at Plymouth Rock. In North America, too, Hispanics established the first permanent settlement, San Agustín, now Saint Augustine, Florida.
- A Latina, the Spanish queen, *la reina Isabel,* became the first hugely successful venture capitalist when she commissioned Cristóbal Colón to seek overseas markets for Spanish wares.
- Spanish gold was the first legal tender in the original thirteen colonies.
- Our forefathers named cities across America: San Antonio, Los Angeles, San Francisco, Sacramento, Las Vegas, Toledo—and fifteen hundred more.

And remember, Latinos in Latin countries excel at running businesses; many do so here. Yet in the corporate world, or in entrepreneurships that have allowed so many immigrants from other ethnic groups to rise to the top levels of business, we seem to fall back or be left out. Although we represent ten percent of the U.S. population, Hispanic businesses generate less than one-half of one percent of all U.S. business revenues.

Can we change this? Is there a realistic way of getting our fair share? I believe—I *know*—there is. That is why I've written *The Americano Dream.*

I was born in San Antonio. My father ran a laundry and dry-cleaning business, working from 7 A.M. to 7 P.M. six days a week, and to my knowledge never missed a day. The family lived in rooms in back of the shop. At an early age I learned to press and sew—I'm still good at those jobs—and quickly recognized the value of hard work.

Even though my father had many Anglo customers ("Cater to the gringo," he advised, *"así es como se hace el dinero"*—that's the way you make real money) with whom I came in contact, I did not learn English until I was six, attending a mostly German and very Anglo Catholic school near our house. I think my first sentence in English was "I have to go to the bathroom."

As a kid I learned about prejudice, too. My brothers and I were always turned away, for example, from a beautiful public park in the then all-Anglo community of New Braunfels, a few miles north of San Antonio. And I still remember with sadness seeing a sign at a restaurant that read NO DOGS, NIGGERS OR MEXICANS ALLOWED.

Prejudice also occurs in business, I would learn. Many of us have encountered it so frequently that we expect it to be present in the corporate world. But "they don't like Latinos" is often a too-easy rationalization for giving up. Prejudice does not crop up nearly as often as some Latinos think. Business is, after all, about making money. If you can help a business make money, it's amazing how quickly prejudice vanishes.

Most of my early training was at an all-Mexican junior high and high school where well-intentioned teachers prepared us to be "good with our hands." My skill was in commercial art and design. There was no thought of any other kind of education. Mexicans simply did not go to college. (How's *that* for stereotyping!) If one learned a trade such as auto mechanics, carpentry, or upholstery, the powers that be reasoned, one could clearly "succeed" in adult life.

My first regular job was at a sign manufacturing company, Texas Neon. It was 1959. I was nineteen years old. My salary was $37.50 a week, enough to enable me to get married a year later, have a child, and find myself in debt up to my eyeballs (*hasta el copete*). Five years later, we had four kids, the debt was four times worse, and even though I was now earning $1.75 an hour, we could not keep up with expenses.

I had come to a crossroads, as, I believe, every Latino must. I would either struggle on with a secure (though ill-paying) job, devote myself to my family, muddle through *poco a poquito*—or *change* my life and go into business for myself. Being "Mexican," I knew, imposed cultural and psychological conditions on me I would have to overcome. But I also felt that as a businessman I was first and foremost an American, and thus worthy, like every American, of every success I could achieve.

So thirty-five years ago I became an entrepreneur, *un hombre de negocios.* That's when I set my first goal: to create the largest graphic design studio in Texas.

It took five years—but we did it! And ten years after that goal was reached, I had reached another: to transform the design studio into a full-fledged advertising agency. Our new business was to be a general market agency like the "Anglo agencies." But it was tough to make the conversion. My former clients (mostly advertising agencies) were now my competitors. It was like starting all over again. For several years I and my partners, Guadalupe Garcia and John Witherspoon, struggled to attract new clients. I refused to fire anybody even if I couldn't keep them all busy. I ran up huge debts and took on more partners to keep from going under.

Salvation came from a man by the name of John Tower, just then running for his third term as U.S. senator. He was anxious to gain a larger share of the Hispanic vote which he knew might be crucial in what was projected to be a close election.

We presented our ideas to Tower and his entire staff in Washington, D.C., and, we thought, won the business. But no—Tower's wife hated our designs. We were eliminated from the competition and our jubilation turned to despair. Two weeks later, though, Tower's people came back. It seemed that Mrs. Tower hated the other agencies' plans *more* than ours, and we were on board for one of the most exciting elections in Texas history.

Tower got thirty-seven percent of the Hispanic vote, enough to give him the victory. No previous Republican politician in Texas had ever gotten more than 5 percent. Our agency was on its way. Soon we were doing Hispanic advertising for such blue-chip clients as Bacardi rum, Dr. Pepper, and Coors beer. When I saw the size of the billings (three to ten times bigger than the average of our accounts) I suggested we go exclusively with the large national clients targeting the Hispanic market. To my amazement, my partners balked. They didn't want to be tabbed a "Hispanic agency."

We couldn't agree, so they bought me out in June 1980 and I started my own firm, Sosa and Associates. My next clear goal was to make ours a Latino-only agency, working with U.S. corporations that needed to attract the Latino market.

Again, my first major client was a politician, drawn to me by my success with Senator Tower—a fellow named Ronald Reagan. His marketing coordinator came to San Antonio, and we constructed a series of radio and television ads in Spanish which aired in Texas and California, stressing family values, an appeal we knew would suit the Latino audience. "You may not know it," the ads said, "but you are conservative in your values and think like a Republican. Ronald Reagan believes what you believe. We both believe in individual opportunity based on our own initiative. We believe in the work ethic, in family values, and in our faith."

The campaign worked. Reagan hired us again in 1984, and George Bush hired us in 1988. We were hugely successful. Our agency reached billings of forty million dollars a year and we were on our way to becoming one of the country's top three! In 1990, I sold forty-nine percent of the agency to my partners and to D'Arcy Masius Benton & Bowles for enough money to guarantee my financial security for a lifetime.

But I kept dreaming, kept setting goals. I am now in the process of fulfilling my next great goal: to create a multicultural advertising agency with Kathy, my wife and partner. Our aim is to serve our clients in a changing America by targeting *all* the ethnic market groups—Latino, African-American, and Asian.

My purpose in writing this book is to share my almost forty years of business experience with you. You will learn from my success and from the success of dozens of Latinos who have made it big in every field. You'll learn lessons that apply to those of you eager to climb to the top of the business ladder. You'll learn from my failures, too; my mistakes have been as profound as any man's. As the great black writer James Baldwin said, that's the price of the ticket.

Still, until recently, my success was not as sweet as it should have been. For years I felt I didn't *deserve* my success. For far too long I didn't feel equal to the Anglos with whom I was doing business. Ah, the internal demons that impede the pleasure of success! *Appreciate* yourself. This seems to be tough for most people, and even harder for Latinos—which would imply that there are few successful Latinos.

Yet there are thousands. In national government, Henry Bonilla is an influential new congressman, Henry Cisneros rose to be Secretary of Housing and Urban Development, then on to become president of Univision, the nation's most successful Spanish-language television network, Federico Peña was Secretary of Transportation and is now Secretary of Energy, Jose Martinez was a special advisor to George Bush, MariCarmen Aponte is one of President Clinton's advisors, Antonia Novello was President Bush's Surgeon General, Loretta Sanchez is a newly elected congresswoman from California. (Latina women's rise to success has been slower and even more difficult than Latino men's, though things are looking up. I've devoted a chapter to this unacceptable phenomenon.) Roberto Goizueta is chairman of Coca-Cola worldwide, Eduardo Caballero has made millions as a Spanish-language media mogul, Ric Cervera made three million dollars by the time he was thirty-eight running the fast-food chain Taco Cabana. Dr. Louis Agnese was voted one of the Ten Outstanding People of the World by the Jaycees. Nely Galan is a top producer of television shows in Hollywood. Rita Moreno, Gloria Estefan, Jennifer Lopez, Geraldo Rivera, Edward James Olmos, Andy Garcia, Jimmy Smits—all are major stars.

I know some of these people personally, and I tell their stories in the pages that follow. You'll find aspects common to them all that you may share as well. And you'll find the means for success in both general and individual terms—practical advice on such matters as planning, communication, negotiation; the way to transform our heritage and our deepest values into invaluable tools for success. By the time you've finished, you'll know how to compete—and win—in American business and American society.

You can overcome your inhibitions, push away your insecurities, compete on an equal level, and prosper proportionately. I've mapped out that road for you because I've traveled it myself. I've overcome the odds you'll face, experienced the problems unique to Latinos in the Anglo business world, trained myself to face the psychological and sociological stumbling blocks that impede Latino progress. I've learned to compete, learned to *win*.

With all due modesty, I am considered one of the most successful Latino entrepreneurs in the United States by both Latinos and Anglos. I've served on the boards of banks and universities; I've chaired the United Way of San Antonio and the San Antonio Symphony Orchestra; I lecture all over the country and have appeared on countless radio and television shows, both national and local. I'm financially secure enough to retire whenever I want to. I'm a friend of corporate executives, movie stars, presidents.

I tell you this not to boast but to prove that a Latino can rise to the top of the American business world. My story is one of hard work, energy, ambition, aggressiveness, stick-to-itiveness, *huevos*.

Mine could be the story of any Latino, man or woman, and in living it I've realized that success is valueless if it is not shared. *The Americano Dream* is my way of sharing. As a Latino—and as an American businessman.

One last thing: Sometimes to make a point, my examples may come off to some readers as insensitive, stereotypical, and/or judgmental. If I offend you, I apologize in advance.

CHAPTER 1

ESCAPING THE CULTURAL SHACKLES

¿Quién eres tú?

Every time I heard a depressing new statistic on the state of the Hispanic in the United States, every time I saw a new "Hispanics and poverty" headline, I got angry. "This makes no sense at all" I would shout. "How the hell do they gather this data anyway? They must be nuts!" People within earshot thought *I* was nuts the way I carried on.

Well, after some homework, I found out, to my dismay, that the people who wrote these stories aren't crazy—that numbers don't lie. Here's the situation, looking at raw percentages. Proportionately:

- Fewer Latinos are getting educated
- More are living in poverty
- Fewer are getting into white collar jobs
- Fewer are moving up in corporations
- Fewer are succeeding in big business
- More Latino kids are in gangs and in prisons.

Given the Latino's strong work ethic—our strong sense of family and of community—these figures don't compute. Latinos are as smart as anyone. We *care* as much as anyone. Latinos *want success* as much as anyone. Indeed for generations we have risked our lives and futures pursuing the American dream.

So what's the deal? I believe the problem has two parts. The first half of the problem is the uneven playing field—the discrimination, racism, bigotry, and stereotyping. The second and more important half of the problem is the half we *can* do something about. I call it the "Latino disconnect"—our complete lack of awareness of our roots and how they impede our success—a phenomenon that has been largely unexplored.

As much as African Americans, we are slaves. No, we weren't kidnaped and brought here against our will, but we were made slaves just the same. By our Spanish conquerors who colonized our land and raped the Indian women and created the mestizo—the "Hijos de la Chingada," as Octavio Paz observed, "the bastard children of that violation." That status set the tone for our behavior.

The Spanish taught us subservience in the name of good manners. "Como usted mande" (as you command), we replied. It didn't stop there. If we questioned their ways we were referred to *their* Spanish priests, who "in the name of God" set us straight. "To be poor," they preached, "is to deserve heaven. To be rich is to deserve hell. It is good to suffer in this life because in the next life you will find an eternal reward."

Education? "That's not for you," they said. "The girls don't really need it—they'll get married anyway. And the boys? It's better they go to work—to help the family. Work is true virtue."

The way I see it, the Spanish conquerors deliberately created an oppressed underclass whose collective psyche became rooted in passivity and underachievement. And now, we carry these injured psyches across the border to compete in a gringo world rooted in *over*achievement. Is it any wonder then that we trip up time and again trying to make it to the top? Is it any wonder that we don't question the system, that we quickly succumb to authority, that we don't fight for our piece of the pie?

Like every other immigrant, we came to this land of opportunity expecting success. Instead we found barriers we never expected—cultural barriers that keep us falling farther and farther behind.

Let me give you an example of how this conditioning, passed on from countless generations, manifests itself in contemporary life.

Two Los Angeles printers have just received a request to submit a proposal to a publisher who needs color work done for a new series of nature magazines. One is Joe Gomez, whose father came to L.A. from Mexico City in 1949, shortly before Joe was born. The other is Robert Masur, whose father immigrated to America from Leipzig, Germany, just before the start of World War II. Gomez and Masur both want the job, they are equally qualified, and the winner will perform the job with distinction.

In most cases, Masur will get the job—not because the buyer is prejudiced, not because Gomez speaks with an accent (though he does; he and his parents speak only Spanish at home), indeed not because of any factor (including price) other than the buyer's unbiased evaluation of the two applicants.

Here's how they prepared for the presentation and conducted themselves when the presentation took place:

Masur spent two weeks studying everything he could about the publisher, then put together a written proposal specifying delivery dates and costs, describing the "extras" he could provide, and including many examples of his previous work. His knowledge of printing was already secure, but this could be his first big break, so he read a book on presentation skills and rehearsed the entire presentation with a friend, writing and rewriting the proposal until it was razor-sharp. He knew in his heart that he was "the right man for the job"—in fact, he looked at it as a stepping-stone to other large contracts from national publishers—and when he was introduced to the publisher herself, he shook hands firmly and looked her directly in the eye.

He made his presentation, was courteous but not diffident, and answered each question in a firm, assured tone. When he didn't know the answer to a particular question, he said, "I don't know, but I'll find out in two days and get back to you." He had learned what fees other similar printing jobs paid, and when the subject of his own fees came up, he named a competitive price.

When the questions stopped, he rose quickly, shook hands firmly, asked when he might expect to get an answer, thanked the publisher for her time and interest, and left briskly, without looking back.

"I think it went well," he told his wife that evening. "I hope so," she said. "You deserve it."

Gomez's approach was different. The first thought that entered his mind when he heard of the opportunity was "Why are they asking *me* to bid on this job? I don't even know them. They probably have a minority quota to fill." He too was secure in his knowledge of printing, and he too brought examples of his best work to the publisher, but he didn't prepare a written proposal. "My work should speak for itself," he felt, "and besides, if I get it, I get it. If I don't, I don't." He too found out as much as he could about the publisher, studying other magazines she had produced, but allowed himself no time to rehearse his presentation; in fact, he was reluctant to do so. "They've probably already made the decision to hire someone else. Besides, I'm not sure I'm ready for such a big piece of business," he thought. "Maybe I should stick to my Latino clients." With these misgivings, he went to the interview.

He entered the publisher's office diffidently, shook hands, and waited until she was seated before sitting himself. He treated her with enormous politeness, calling her "ma'am" at every opportunity, and, rather than stressing his achievements, chose to be modest. When it came to payment, he found the question somewhat embarrassing, asked her to name her budget, and promised he'd stay within it. As he left, he reiterated what an honor it was to have been interviewed. He did not ask when he might expect an answer, and went home thinking that probably the job would be given to someone else—an "Anglo firm"—even though he knew he was qualified.

"I don't think she likes Latinos," he told his wife that evening. "You're right," his wife said, "but don't worry. You already have plenty of work to do." They were both pleased that he had acted in just the right manner.

⌐

If you are honest with yourself, you will agree that these two stories ring true. And it's not because Joe Gomez is "incompetent" or "inferior" that he did not get the job. It's because his background is different, his heritage is different, his upbringing is different, his manners are different, and so is the way he looks at himself and at the world. It was his *attitude* that influenced the publisher, an attitude shaped by his culture, honed by his parents, and inculcated by years of doing business with Latino-only firms.

One of the most famous Spanish-language movies is the 1953 *Nosotros los pobres*, starring Pedro Infante. An actor of enormous charm, Infante here plays a *peón*, a man not only poor by birth but a continual victim of circumstances. By the end of the film he has lost all: His son is dead; his house has burned down; his wife, unable to cope, has left him.

Among Mexicans the film is considered classic, a representation of the epitome of the Latino soul. Why? Because we have been conditioned to believe that there is virtue in suffering, and to expect a hard but honest road, a life of stoicism in the face of disaster. In a way, we revel in these shackles; they are our comfort zone, and to some extent they are part of all Latinos' makeup.

But they can be overcome, they don't have to constrict our lives. Suffering is a place you might want to visit—but, as my friend Father Virgil Elizondo says, you don't have to stay there. You can of course be virtuous and poor, but you can be virtuous and rich, too—and do far more to benefit your neighbors, your family, and yourself.

At one time or another I've heard all of the following habitual phrases from Latinos who consciously wished to succeed and subconsciously didn't, whose ambivalence stemmed from a clash between the opportunities they saw in the *over*achieving American business culture and the heritage they "saw" in their mind's eye—the heritage of slavery and self-abnegation, which promotes *under*achievement.

"I'm Hispanic. I'm different. I look different. I talk different."
"Being poor is virtuous."
"Whatever will be, will be. It's God's will."
"I'm a minority. That means people see me as second class."
"My parents were not educated."

"My parents don't speak good English."

"I'm not comfortable with my accent."

"I didn't finish high school."

"I never went to college."

"Being humble is virtuous."

"Rich people are unhappy."

"Ambition is not a virtue. It is really greed."

"Pride is not a virtue. It is really ego."

"Any honest job is honorable."

"Sweat is a measure of a good, honest day's work."

"As long as my kids stay out of trouble, that's all I ask for."

"Thank God for a roof over my head and three meals a day."

"I may not have accomplished much, but who cares?"

The important issue isn't whether or not we've said these things, or even felt them. It's that they're mostly not true.

⌐

Two major forces hold us Latinos back in business: the values taught by our own families and the values taught by our church.

"But wait!" you'll say. "Family and church are precisely the forces in our lives that are strongest." True, but you must realize that the "truths" that priests and parents have inculcated in our psyche may not be the absolute truth.

I've been to countless Masses in both Anglo and Latino communities (I still go every Sunday), and the message I hear in each setting is radically different, yet it emanates from fundamentally the same church, the same Catholicism. One says there is hope, the other says subservience is a virtue. Latinos, especially in Mexico, Central America, and the northern cone of South America, where the *indio* was enslaved by Spanish conquerors, have historically been taught to be subservient. Our *"sí, señor,"* and *"mándeme"* are akin to the black slave's "yassuh, massa," the conditioned response when his name was called. After all, a slave is a slave, whether black or brown.

"Whatever will be, will be," Latinos are told. "It is God's will— *lo que quiera Dios.*" Latinos believe this. It is drilled into us by our parents, who learned it from their own parents the Indian slaves of the *conquistadores,* and by our priests, who learned it from their own priests. Indeed, it's as though Latinos follow a kind of heavenly marketing plan:

- Goal: *Lo que Dios quiera*—whatever God wants
- Strategy: *Como Dios quiera*—however God wants it
- Measurement of success: *Así lo quiere Dios*—that's the way God wants it

This kind of teaching worked very well—for the Spaniards. It kept the *indio* right where they wanted him, as a slave, and all in the name of goodness and God. This is the morality taught to the oppressed to keep them quiet and "content." Individual initiative, achievement, self-reliance, ambition, aggressiveness—all these are useless in the face of an attitude that says, We must not challenge the will of God (the will, of course, of the Spanish "God *a la castellana*").

The virtues so essential to business success in the United States are looked upon as sins by the Latino church. *"Es muy ambicioso"*—he's too ambitious—is interpreted as criticism, not praise. *Orgullo,* pride, can mean snobbishness, false pride. Having too much pride in an accomplishment is a sign of arrogance in the face of the church, which has spent centuries extolling humility and acceptance of one's lot. It's okay not to accomplish, not to succeed, we are told. To be aggressive means you are not virtuous, for being aggressive might mean pushing others aside. It might make us rich or successful, and we mere mortals should not covet riches or success. Again, note how such teaching works to keep ambition at bay. Poverty is a virtue because it means that you will suffer, and those who suffer are more welcome in heaven. To dare to shape God's will is not to be contemplated. To be loyal to God you must be subservient to Him. *"Yo no soy digno"*—I'm not worthy—*"soy un pobre humilde"* is a catchphrase Latinos learn early on. (I *still* have moments when the feeling sweeps over me. For years I felt not pleasure but uneasiness when a business venture paid off for me. It was as though I was "not worthy" to receive it.)

In the little villages of Mexico, churches are filled with Sunday worshippers who constantly hear that working with their hands is the greatest virtue, that they are poor but honest, that they should remain content with their lifelong poverty, that there is no other course in this life, and that "happiness" is reserved for the life to come. I want to interrupt the sermon and shout to the priest: "Stop! Why are you doing this? Why do you want to make us believe we are destined to live in poverty?"

In Anglo Catholic churches I've never heard a "poverty is virtue" sermon. Their message is different. Virgil Elizondo, the former rector of San Fernando Cathedral in San Antonio, a learned man who speaks five languages and has two doctorates, is an unusual Latino priest. He preaches that our people deserve anything we want to achieve. Wealth, power, luxuries—we are deserving of all, as long as we use what we have to help others and we hurt no one in our quest for them. He believes, as I do, that instead of leaving everything in God's hands, we must also use our own to better ourselves.

Ambition is a virtue, pride in our own accomplishments an appropriate emotion. We are God's creatures, and He did not create us to be slaves. If we lead moral, honest, virtuous, upstanding lives we will be welcome in the Kingdom of Heaven—rich as well as poor.

The obvious lesson is that if you want to be a successful entrepreneur, you'll have to stop being subservient and learn to take things in your own hands. Doing so is both permissible and essential. You'll have to be innovative, assertive, even aggressive; you'll have to challenge the system, fight for yourself, compete, out-hustle and outwit. Successful Anglo businesspeople do these things routinely, and as long as they do not cheat, lie, mislead, or willfully cause harm to anyone else, I suggest you use them as your models. Compete fairly with them, and you will often find that what you took as "prejudice" is merely the *instilled* feeling that you're not up to their level.

In 1985 I made a presentation to Coca-Cola in an effort to win their account. The man in charge of ethnic advertising, Chuck Morrison, turned out to be African-American, and when I first saw him I admit I was taken aback. I was used to dealing with Anglos, but I knew nothing about African-Americans and didn't really think about them much. I felt ill at ease, not sure what to expect.

What I *got* was a brilliant man who not only knew his business but helped me plot our marketing strategies—then and over the years. It didn't take me too long to realize I needed this black man if I wanted more business. He was my boss, and he could open new doors of opportunity for me. He did open those doors, and he became a trusted friend. I discovered that our family backgrounds, and our cultural experiences, had many more similarities than differences. It quickly became apparent that in matters of business, and in the bonds that tie people together, we are alike. We are all family.

⤳

¡Familia! No one values it more than Latinos; no one fights harder to maintain its unity, to protect its members, to cherish its traditions.

Estimable virtues, and very much to be admired and upheld. But when it comes to business, often a roadblock.

Latinos rely on family. Husbands, wives, children, parents, grandparents: these are the people we trust, the people we want in business with us. The father expects his son or daughter to learn the business from him, so that he will leave them something after he dies. Indeed, the passing down of the "family business" is the cornerstone of Latino economic life—promising *una vida mejor que lo que yo tuve* (a better life than I've had)—but it is not always the right road for the entrepreneur.

Our families stick together, both emotionally and physically. We are loath to move from one city to another, even when opportunity beckons, if it means leaving family members (parents, brothers and sisters, aunts and uncles) behind. Latino students are likely to go to a nearby college, even if their grades qualify them for finer universities sometimes thousands of miles away.

A family—let's name them Morales—started a small restaurant in the Spanish section of Albuquerque. It quickly became popular, since Mrs. Morales was an inspired cook and her husband a charming host. Their daughter helped her mother in the kitchen; their son, still in high school, was the lone waiter. Because there were only a few tables, and because they kept their prices low, their profits were not great. The work hours were horrendous, and Mr. Morales was uncomfortably aware that the labor of keeping the books, buying the food, and acting as captain was getting to him. He was tired all the time.

An Anglo restaurateur who knew of the restaurant's fine reputation stopped in for a meal, returned for another, and then approached Mr. Morales with a business proposition: If Mrs. Morales agreed to stay on as cook and Mr. Morales as captain, he would move the restaurant to a downtown location, vastly increase its seating space, cater to a primarily Anglo clientele, and open for lunch as well as dinner. He would hire as much help as Mrs. Morales needed, the daughter could stay or not as she pleased, the son would be free to spend his nights on homework. All this he was willing to finance. Mr. Morales would bear none of the financial risks, and he would get twenty-five percent of the profits.

Mr. Morales never really considered the offer. He turned him down flat. The Anglo was a nice enough fellow, Morales confided to his wife, but "Who knows what this man's real motives are? He'll probably take over, and before we know it we'll lose everything." Besides, they were comfortable where they were, they knew their patrons, the restaurant was family owned and family run, a fitting inheritance for their children. What's more, Morales said, his brother Diego had approached him that very week, looking for a job. Diego was a bookkeeper! He could keep the accounts, negotiate with the wholesalers, remove a huge burden from Morales's back. And Diego was *familia*! He could be trusted.

Indeed Diego was trustworthy. He was a good man, but also not the best man for the job. He made mistakes in the accounts and was overcharged by the wholesalers. Though Diego tried hard and was sincerely apologetic for his mistakes, Morales had to make him an *ayudante*, a helper. Since Diego was family, Morales couldn't fire him, so he simply took back his old duties, now with an extra salary to pay.

The Moraleses' restaurant is still a popular eating place; in fact, it's twice its former size. But now Morales, a little older and a bit more tired, has most of the family working for him, labors just as hard as he ever did, and earns no more than he did years ago.

I have a friend who counsels Latino high school students on job training. He begins his lectures by writing two sentences on a blackboard and asking the students to pick one of them:

1. I will be successful in life.
2. I will not be very successful in life.

If you pick 1, he tells the students, you are correct. If you pick 2, you are also correct. For you become what you believe. Believe you'll be successful, and you will be. Believe you will not, and you will not be. That truth is at the basis of all achievement, or the lack of it.

All of us—Anglo, Latino, Asian, African—consciously or unconsciously place ourselves somewhere on the line between success and failure in virtually everything we do.

We Latinos think we're successful parents, poets, mechanics, carpenters, musicians, cooks, baseball players, teachers, and yes, lovers. We thrive on family unity, love of country, a strong work ethic. We believe in God and *la Virgencita*. These are significant values, and we must never abandon them.

But when it comes to business we too often blink. We hesitate. We remind ourselves of the things we don't deserve. We conclude that servility is required for survival. We quickly believe you have to "know your place"—*tienes que saber tu lugar*—and our place is not at the top.

Most Latinos in the United States believe this, though not the *cubanos*, most of whom, well educated, fled here to escape Castro—not because they were looking for a better way of life (they already had it) but to avoid the repression of a Communist government. I joke to friends that I never met a Cuban in the United States with an inferiority complex and I've rarely met a Mexican who didn't have one. The European Latinos—the descendants of Spanish and Portuguese—are also very confident people. It's only the *mestizos* (that is, the Latinos who are a mix of a little European and a lot of *indio*—me included) who are "subservient." But we make up more than 85 percent of the U.S. Hispanic population.

The story of my friend Eduardo Caballero is illustrative of a *cubano* immigrant's success. In pre-Castro Cuba, he and his wife Raquel were successful lawyers in their twenties and had amassed a fair amount of savings, all of which they lost, along with their house and practice, when Castro took over. They came to the United States with one dollar Eduardo had hidden in his sock and the clothes they were wearing, and were taken in by cousins in Miami. For a time Eduardo waited tables to pay for his keep. But even though he missed his homeland, his eye was on the future, not the past. He had a goal. "We're going to make back that half million, and millions more," he told Raquel. "I don't quite know how yet, but somehow or other, we'll do it." She agreed—in fact, encouraged him vigorously.

Eventually they moved to New York and he got a job selling advertising space for a Spanish-language radio station. He was able to attract a number of advertisers and, buoyed by his success, approached other Spanish-language stations across the country, in effect becoming their "sales force on Madison Avenue." He bought their unsold airtime at bargain prices, and when he had more than a hundred of them lined up, he went to a number of Fortune 500 companies with a proposition. "Advertise with me," he told them. "I can give you a package of one hundred stations, nationwide coverage in the Latino market. You don't have to advertise piecemeal. I can offer you a marvelous price, you'll only have to prepare one ad, you'll get only one invoice, and your coverage will be extensive."

The companies bought—and, finding their sales increasing, bought again and again. Eduardo and Raquel became business partners. They earned a half million in commissions and went on to make millions more. Do they consider themselves members of a minority? Sure, but they know they're the equal of any Anglo. Do they believe they deserve their success? You bet they do!

To achieve his goal, Eduardo used aggressiveness and initiative, along with an utter lack of self-pity. He had no sense of inferiority, no feeling that he was "not good enough." There was no chip on his shoulder, only ambition in his heart.

To succeed in business—indeed, in life—we Latinos need more of the positive traits exemplified by Eduardo, and as I go around the country, I see that in fact more and more of us (though by no means enough) have these traits.

Take Congressman Henry Bonilla, for example. Brought up in San Antonio in a poor, extraordinarily close family, Henry had never been more than a hundred miles from home until after he graduated from the University of Texas at Austin. Throughout his childhood his "window on the world" was television, which he watched incessantly. "*I* can work in television," he thought, and his dad agreed. "If you want something, you can get it. If you think you can do it, do it!" Henry had a goal: to be the top producer of news programs for the most important TV station in America—at the time, WABC in New York.

His first full time job was as a reporter at a small NBC affiliate in Austin, Texas. He quickly moved up the ladder to KENS-TV in San Antonio, the top-rated CBS affiliate in the country at the time. It was at this television station where he finally moved to producing full time on the highest rated 10 o'clock news. Soon thereafter, he and his wife, Deborah, moved to Philadelphia, where she had landed a job as a prime-time anchor.

Focused on his goal, he went directly to New York (close enough to Philadelphia to commute) and was hired on the spot by WABC as a news writer. Soon, however, his boss called him on the carpet. "You're not cutting it," he was told.

"What am I doing wrong?"

"Your stories are too long. You're not getting to the fundamentals. Stick to the basics. Write declarative sentences with a beginning, middle, and end."

The criticism did not faze him. He just took the advice and imporved his performance. He came up with the idea for a special series, *How to Be a More Interesting Person*, which became so popular that WABC featured it in their ads for the nightly news program. The series also helped the television station win a critical ratings war. Within six months he was producing the 11 o'clock news on weekends. Six months later he was producing the weeknight 11 o'clock news, with an average audience of two million people. He had reached his goal: by age thirty, he was producer of the number one news show in the biggest television market in America. (Tom Snyder was the anchorman; after a difficult start, he and Henry became great friends.) Not bad for a Mexican kid from a poor neighborhood.

After four and a half years in the East, tired of commuting, he and Deborah moved back to San Antonio, she to become anchorwoman for KENS-TV, he to become its executive producer for news and public affairs. Then Henry decided to run for Congress in 1992. With no experience but with the same drive and aggressiveness he had shown at WABC, he beat a formidable incumbent by twenty percent of the vote and went to Washington to become one of the most influential freshmen in the Congress, so popular that Newt Gingrich asked him to give the nominating speech when Gingrich ran for Speaker of the House.

To me, the meaning of Henry's history is threefold: First, that if you know *exactly* what you want, you'll get it. Second, that you must put up oftentimes with adverse conditions (initial hostility, living where you feel uncomfortable) to achieve your goal. Third, that Latino-ness is not a determining factor. Henry did not become a top producer *even though* he was Mexican (though being Latino probably helped him in his congressional race). He got the job because he proved he was the best man for it.

⤳

I believe that if you tell yourself, "I am worthy, I *deserve* success, *yo soy digno*," several times a day every day for a year—that is, keep it always in your conscious mind—your unconscious mind, your *soul*, will come to believe it.

Still, for Latinos it's a struggle. For me, many times, it has been a struggle.

Just before Ronald Reagan's campaign for a second term, I had been appointed an advisor to the President on the Hispanic electorate. An aide of his with whom I was working asked me a question that touched on my feelings of worth.

"What if President Reagan asked you to the White House to talk to you about the ads?" the advisor asked.

"I'd be delighted to go!" I said with great confidence.

"But what if he just wanted to sit down and chat with you for an hour. Just talking about you?"

I could feel my face redden at the prospect. I was over-whelmed. Why would he want to talk to me about *me*? Why should he care? What would I say?

All of us, I suppose, have gone into meetings or been in social situations where we feel uneasy, as though we did not belong. We want to escape, hide under the couch, excuse ourselves by having "another commitment," and then rush to our familiar, nonthreat-ening home.

The only thing to do at such times is to be aware that we are having these feelings, *sit through* the feelings, and face them squarely. They'll pass if we let them surface and don't deny them, and if you remember that each person at the meeting, every guest at the party, has at one time or another experienced similar feelings. Everyone has had moments of awkwardness, of self-doubt. Everyone at one time or another has felt unworthy, re-gardless of background or color.

But the fact is that we Latinos *are* just as worthy as anyone to compete, to succeed, to win. *Somos iguales*—we're equals. The en-trepreneur must consider his ancestry as a point of pride, use his Latino-ness as an asset and his heritage as a foundation for self-confidence. Pride in oneself and one's people is an essential ele-ment of self-confidence. In the following chapters, I'll show you how to gain that self-confidence, discover your own sense of self, and then translate that newfound dignity into business success.

Remember, our Spanish conquerors for their own benefit de-liberately created an oppressed underclass whose collective psy-che became rooted in passivity and underachievement. We must free ourselves of these cultural shackles. For they exist alright, but only in our minds. The first step toward our freedom is recog-nizing that we alone have the key that unlocks them. All we have to do is use our desire to win to turn the key.

CHAPTER 2

THE TRAIN IS MOVING—ARE YOU ON BOARD?

¿Te subes o te quedas?

It's a great time to be an American Hispanic. Look at what's happening right now:

- There are more Hispanics (over thirty million) in the United States than there are Canadians in Canada.
- If American Hispanics formed a Latin American country, we would be the fifth largest—and by far the richest.
- By 2010, Hispanics will be the largest minority group in the United States.
- Even without a quota system, colleges and universities feel a moral and intellectual obligation to attract minority groups—and Hispanics achieve a better than average academic record once they enroll.
- Most Latinos live in Texas, California, Florida, New York, New Jersey, and Illinois. These are the states with the largest number of electoral votes (210—only 60 short of the number needed to be president), and my own work for Tower, Reagan, and Bush has shown how dramatically powerful a

political group we are. Latino voter registration is expanding exponentially. Half a million more Latinos voted in 1996 than in 1992. In the year 2000 the Latino vote will almost surely be a decisive factor in who gets to be president. In 1996 it helped to determine several congressional races.

- American Latinos have almost four hundred billion dollars of expendable income. No wonder this huge consumer market is increasingly a target for, among others, all Fortune 500 companies.

- American corporations now spend more than two billion dollars to reach this market, and that number will double in less than five years.

- American Hispanics will more and more play a role in Latin America, since Latin American firms are increasingly anxious to adopt American business practices—and who better to help them?

- By 2050, Asians, African-Americans, Hispanics, and other "non-whites" will form fifty percent of the U.S. population.

- As we continue on the trend toward the "browning" of America, Hispanics will be hired in ever-increasing numbers.

- Indeed, American firms are already recruiting heavily at such schools as UCLA, Harvard, the University of Miami, and Michigan.

- Hispanic contributions to the arts, government, politics, sports, and business—to every sphere of American life—are taken for granted. No one says, "That's remarkably good work *for a Latino*." We are *expected* to do good work. That we succeed is a given.

The train is on the track and running. It has unlimited room and unlimited cars. It is accelerating and will go even faster in the coming years. But it will never go so fast that we cannot get on.

⌐

"Is the train for me?" we ask. "I'm glad it's there, I hope my friends and colleagues ride on it, but me—*¿qué ago yo?*

"What if I get on and then fall off? What if it takes me to a foreign land where I know no one, can't speak the language, have no map to help me when I'm lost? What if I don't have the right ticket? What if all the other passengers deserve to be on board and I don't?"

After all, there *is* still discrimination in many parts of America. (The welfare bill passed in 1996, with its punitive stance toward *legal* immigrants, is testament to that, since these days the vast majority of immigrants are Latino.) Yes, there are company CEOs (and heads of country clubs) who don't even *look* at Hispanics, let alone allow them to work or play comfortably on their territory. And it's still true that to some Anglos darker skin or any accent means "foreign," and "foreign" means "outsider." Stereotypes exist, fostered by the depiction of Latinos in movies and television (endearing, but not very bright). Many Latinos are still pressed into below-minimum-wage migrant jobs. Domestic work, garden work, fruit picking are considered "fitting" for Hispanics, as long as we know our place.

So it's natural for us to feel unworthy at worst, wary at best. Yet our first step toward boarding the train (or at least getting to the platform) is to recognize these feelings—*saber sentir*—and acknowledge they exist. For only by recognition and acceptance can we overcome them, and only by overcoming them can we get on board.

Psychologist and family counselor Irv Loev argues that what motivates most people to succeed in business is fear: fear of failure, fear of poverty, fear of society's scorn, fear of being thought "second class," fear of not maintaining the standard of "keeping up with the Joneses" like their parents and grandparents. But these are *Anglo* fears. They are not necessarily held by Latinos.

To many Anglos, failure can often mean *monetary* failure—simply not making enough to live as one wants. I've heard executives earning half a million dollars a year complain that they're falling behind, just because their friends are earning a million. Poverty, too, has myriad meanings. Everyone fears going without food or shelter, but Anglos take it much further. Many of them think they're "deprived" if they can't afford a new car every three years. If they can't keep up with their peers, they imagine they're scorned (they probably are, at least by some) and see themselves as second class. *Real* successes go first class.

When the Puritans, driven by religious persecution, came to America in the seventeenth and eighteenth centuries, they found an often harsh land, enemies in the indigenous population—and virtually unlimited opportunity. Through hard work and more hard work they built farms, roads, cities, communities, a Great Society. And they left a legacy of overachievement that to an Anglo is almost unshakable. "America is number one."

Think of the shibboleths the present-day puritans live by:

"Don't waste time."

"Time is money."

"Idle hands are the Devil's tools."

"Don't put off till tomorrow what you can do today."

"A penny saved is a penny earned."

"You've come a long way, baby—and can go further still."

"The American Dream is yours for the taking."

"You can have it all."

"Just do it."

Today it's considered a virtue to "multitask"—do several jobs at the same time. Faxes, voice mail, E-mail, laser-speed, cutting-edge digital technology, everything in the name of success, material success. His computer can talk to her computer while the human beings are off on a management retreat, *working*, trying to figure out why profits this quarter fell .05 percent below the comparable period last year.

Boomers and Generation Xers take cellular phones to the beach, fax messages to the office from a restaurant in Paris, take pictures of an Uxmal pyramid without getting out of their car. (I actually saw this happen. *Me voló el coco*—it blew my mind.)

This is not making fun of success, just the excesses "Americans" go to in its name. There is of course a middle road possible between work and family, stress and relaxation, ambition and altruism, the worshipping of God and the worshipping of money. And Latinos, it seems to me, are in a unique position to find that middle road and define it.

~

Latinos do not have the fears that drive Anglos toward success.

Poverty? Our church teaches us that poverty is a blessing.

Failure? We have not failed if we have provided food and shelter for our family.

Society's scorn? We have experienced so much, it no longer seems pernicious. And if we accept it as our lot, the fear of failure and poverty diminishes still further.

Second class status? Why, we see it all around us and too often take it for granted. When was the last time a Latino hired an Anglo to mow his lawn, a Latina employed an Anglo as a nanny?

We do not come from a puritan tradition, and so do not share the overachieving ethic it engendered. Our roots, like the African-Americans', lie in slavery, so we expect to work manually, to earn our living by the sweat of our brow and the muscle in our back, but we do not feel that doing "better" at these jobs will lead anywhere. *"Qualquier trabajo honesto es trabajo bueno"*—*any* honest job is a good job.

We do the best we can, work as hard as we can, not because we expect any particular material reward (we are, after all, rewarded by God) but because we must survive and provide for our families.

The greatest occasions in our lives—the weddings, funerals, births, feast days, religious holidays—are glorious, elaborate affairs—representative of the balance in Latino life. I don't remember noticing a cellular phone at a Hispanic wedding, or hearing the beep of a pager during Mass.

Latinos have far different fears, and (as already pointed out) rather than spurring us toward success, they sometimes limit our sight to a certain safe point—which, once reached, represents the height of our ambition—and afford us relief as we hesitate, even stop and go no farther.

Almost all Latinos believe success is possible in the United States, *"el país de la oportunidad"*—that's why most of us are here! But our definition of success can be different from an Anglo's, and what for us is the end of the track is only the beginning for them.

Let's examine the Latino fears:

The first is the fear of not being a good provider. In our culture the most important goal—in fact for many the only goal, *lo único*—is to take care of our families, to give them enough food, to provide a decent home. But this honest and basic desire is also a simple desire. Many of us have learned to limit our sights because our culture has systematically quashed our desire for riches, our will to be really successful. So we do not think of "providing" the way an Anglo does. An Anglo wants to provide the trappings of the good life—*cuatro recámaras, tres coches*—the Latino its bare necessities, *solo lo necesario.*

A second fear is the fear of not being a good parent. Our children are our legacy, and for them we want more than we have: a better life, a better education, increased opportunities. To not be able to give them that chance fills us with worry. We will not let it happen! Having our children do better than we do, no matter if it's only *"un poquito mejor,"* is our definition of success.

Yet how frequently we sabotage this natural desire. "What, send our children to a college far away from home? *¡Ni lo mande Dios!*" That would be too lonely for them, and too lonely for us. A real family can only be comfortable surrounded by familiar things, familiar people. Train them for a profession other than our own? Too dangerous. Who knows if they will succeed if we ourselves are not there to teach them? If they work with us at the shop (or, in my case, the laundry), they will make the business grow and in *that* way do better than we have. There is less risk in this route, less of an element of bad luck, a smaller chance that our children will fail. This safety we create around them helps to insure that they will be good providers, and thus not face the cruelty we have so keenly experienced.

Our motives here are good without a doubt—remember, *"así lo quiere Dios."* But there is an unconscious and subversive narcissism at work, a way of saying, "You'll do well but only through me. Only in what I can teach you." The family unit is kept intact; the business will grow slowly but surely; if we train our children to be a slightly better tuned version of ourselves, the tradition endures.

A third fear is the fear of being rejected. Humiliation is anathema to Latinos (it is to everybody, but I truly believe we feel it more acutely than Anglos at least), and to avoid rejection we avoid risk. If we try for a job and are turned down, our egos are severely damaged, and it is unlikely we will try for a similar job when the opportunity arises; *two* rejections would be almost unbearable.

It's why we so often make excuses ("They just don't like Latinos" and "Even though I'm more qualified, the Anglo will get the job") and why we sometimes don't adequately prepare for the interview. If we leave our fate in the hands of God (or in the hands of Anglos), then to be turned down is not really a rejection of ourselves. God has other plans, we tell ourselves. And Anglos don't know who we really are, and it makes no sense to show them, because they're prejudiced against us anyway.

The next fear is the fear of being dominated. The origins of this are easy to trace; no one whose forefather was a slave could conceivably not feel it. But it comes too from the sermons of the priests, who preach against disobeying "God's will," and sometimes even from the nuns who taught us our first lessons, in the old days with a ruler. Our fear, thus, is quite natural. But it has unusual repercussions in the business world.

For one thing, it makes us overly eager to please. If we show ourselves as humble, good workers, noncontroversial, we will be accepted or, better, overlooked. There will be no criticism of our behavior, no harshness from our bosses in their treatment of us. In a way, we choose to dominate ourselves rather than have someone else do it.

To our ancestors, revolution brought repression. To us, revolt—even so minor a one as telling our boss he's wrong when indeed he is—is therefore to be avoided. *Eso es falta de educación*— that would demonstrate a lack of respect, a lack of a proper upbringing. If we disobey, if we protest, if we do not do our job passively, precisely as it has been defined, then we will soon be squashed.

Our fear makes most of us comfortable in a family-owned, family-run business. It's one of the reasons we surround ourselves with those we know best, even though, many times, they might not be best for the job.

We take risks on lotteries but are cautious with our lives. A steady job, a loving family, lots of friends with whom to relax, an elaborate coming-of-age *quinceañera* for our daughters, a place in the business for our sons, a chance to return every so often to our *tierra madre*—mother country. What more could we want?

Well, I say it's okay to want greater success and greater recognition, a success and recognition that will take us above mediocrity, that will make us part of the top five percent of the American population in terms of wealth, a success and recognition that will give us control of our and our children's destiny, a success and recognition that will make us people of influence, able to change not only our own lives but the lives of our compatriots, a success and recognition that will afford us power—political, economic, and social.

This is the train's destination. When you get on, you will find yourselves traveling steadily uphill *hasta el cielo*—toward the heights.

⤳

Fear, of course, is not the only factor that propels Anglos toward success, or the only factor that prevents Latinos from achieving it.

There is ambition, and there are dreams.

From the time I was ten, I had loved to draw and paint. I remember that my glamorous, mysterious uncle, who had been deported from San Antonio to Mexico City for bigamy, would drive up from time to time in his gleaming 1939 Mercedes-Benz and tell me I had "the hands of a great painter." I believed him completely. I sketched people and painted landscapes, still lifes, anything. In seventh grade, for fifty-five blessed minutes a day, my art teacher, Eldah Burke, let me and thirty-one other kids, all Mexican, paint to our hearts' content. She taught four additional hours on Saturday afternoons. I did not miss a session. I was going to be the next Picasso! After all, Tío Fernando had planted the seed; he had "seen" my greatness!

I joined the Marine Corps right after high school, but it became obvious the military was not for me. I felt I was destined to be rich and famous. I knew that if I could put my talent at the service of my great inspiration, Walt Disney, the man who hypnotized me on television every Sunday night, he would hire me. Once he saw my work, how could he not?

I used my off-duty hours at Camp Pendleton, California, to prepare a portfolio of drawings. When I left the service I bought a bus ticket to Burbank, prepared to meet my hero. Alas, a local bus strike made it impossible for me to get to Disney's studio. I couldn't afford a cab, since all the cash I had was for my fare home. So I mailed my portfolio to him, bought my ticket back home, and waited for Disney's offer of employment. (Maybe unconsciously I needed to please Mom and Dad and *regresar a la familia*—come home to the family.)

In two weeks my portfolio came back, with a form rejection signed by someone with an illegible signature. Mr. Disney, it seemed, had no need of my services.

"No hay problema." His loss.

I turned to the best alternative: sign painting. I put out my shingle. SIGNS, it read, and it stood proudly on the front lawn of our house. It was my initial stab at being an entrepreneur, *un hombre de negocios.*

It worked. The sign was noticed by a well-known insurance salesman named O. P. Schnabel, who promoted his business by putting his name on all the trash bins in San Antonio as part of a public keep-our-city-clean service. He would have me paint them with either of two messages. BE A BEAUTY BUG, NOT A LITTER BUG read one. A CLEAN CITY IS A HEALTHY CITY read the other. Then, in smaller letters, "Courtesy O. P. Schnabel, Jefferson Standard Life." I would paint fifteen bins a week at $1.75 a bin. My work was seen all over town. To me, it was like *being* Picasso. There was my work, for all to see—and who cared if it was on trash bins.

But wonderful as the money and exposure were, I needed a regular job and found one at Texas Neon, a sign manufacturing company. I earned enough to put a down payment on a car and, a year later, get married.

At Texas Neon, a gringo named Leonard Dyke became my best friend, *mi íntimo amigo.* He, like my uncle, proved to be a source of inspiration—and of dreams.

"How much do you want to earn?" he asked one day, out of the blue. "A hundred dollars a week? Two hundred? Five?"

I was dumbfounded. "Nowhere near that. Not for a long, long time."

He looked at me with fire in his eyes. "You know," he confided, "there are people no smarter than you right here in this town who earn a thousand a week—even twice that!"

"You're kidding!"

"A thousand. Ten thousand!" He was relentless. "What's more," he added, "thousands of people make that kind of money all around us. *You* can make that kind of money. You have it in you."

I could barely conceive of such sums. But Dyke had planted a second seed in my head. I don't know if you'd call it ambition. (I was already ambitious, only my ambitions were, in Latino fashion, aimed too low—in Burbank, after all, at the first barrier, the bus strike, I gave up and came home.) Rather, the challenge Leonard threw at me hit a nerve, my sense of self-esteem. I had a dream based on a skill, Disney notwithstanding. I could paint canvases and paint signs. I could *use my talents* not only to my satisfaction but to others'—and they would pay me for it.

But money is by no means the only factor that motivates Latinos positively. There are at least five others—and stories to illustrate all of them.

1. Latinos are motivated to prove something. Recently Nely Galan was named by *Entertainment Weekly* as "one of Hollywood's top guns most likely to influence tomorrow's entertainment." (The *New York Times* had already listed her as a "baby mogul" and described her as a "tropical typhoon.")

Nely was born in Cuba, came with her family to America when she was four and, like Henry Bonilla, spent as much of her childhood as she could watching television. It was her "secret garden," for it served as a bridge for her between the Latino and Anglo worlds. Her favorite show was *The Brady Bunch,* her mother's the Spanish-language soap opera *María Teresa,* and Nely dreamed of one day going to Hollywood and making her own show where Marcia Brady and María Teresa could live together.

She began to write and at age fifteen turned in to her teacher an essay so good that the nuns at the Catholic school she attended accused her of plagiarism. "But I wrote it myself," she insisted. "It was stolen," they said, and expelled her.

Nely sent the essay to the editors at *Seventeen* magazine, who liked it so much they hired her as a teenage reporter. She moved to New York at sixteen, became a producer for CBS and PBS—and continued to dream of Hollywood, still as far off as Never-Never-Land. At twenty-two, she took a job in Newark, New Jersey, as general manager (meaning, among other things, producer and talk-show host) of a Spanish-language TV station, where she at last began to "do her thing"—speak to a new generation of Latinos.

She had given up hope of going to Hollywood when, in 1992, HBO hired her to head up her own Latino division. There she worked with every top Hispanic performer. Then in 1994 Fox TV set her up with her own production company, where she could produce and market shows for both the U.S. and Latin America. Where is her production company located? Why, Hollywood, of course!

"I'm going to show those nuns," Nely said early in her life.

She did.

2. *Latinos are motivated to overcome the past.* Johnny Gabriel, whom you'll meet again later in the book, is the foremost liquor retailer in South Texas. His mother owned several bars on the 99 percent Latino west side of San Antonio. She was a street-smart woman, a wheeler-dealer, but Johnny grew up determined to do better. He swore that his wife Rosalee and their children would live in a better place, have a better life. I've never met people who worked more diligently than Johnny and Rosalee toward a single goal, and I watched their liquor stores grow not only in number but in beauty, to the point where he now *owns* the market. His stores have superbly stocked wine cellars and rooms for cigar smoking. Vintners court him. And now that he is so well established, he has turned his attention to spending more time with his family and to community service. A prominent member of the Hispanic Chamber of Commerce, he has also established the Gabriel Scholarship Fund for needy Latino children. He has

taken his family name and honor to a new place. His past is overcome—but not forgotten.

3. Latinos are motivated to win recognition by their peers. Bill Gonzaba had a grand ambition: He wanted to be the best doctor, Latino or Anglo, to serve the Latino community. Starting from an obscure one-person office on San Antonio's south side, he and his wife, an organizational genius, built a series of clinics that soon became famous as places where patients could get the best possible care. Recently he sold the practice he and his wife had built for over $25 million. Last year, the stock options alone netted him an additional five million dollars. Did he prove to his Anglo peers that he was as good or better than any of them? If money is any criteria he sure did. How many other doctors have a nest egg of thirty million? He's certainly the only Latino doctor in San Antonio to achieve it.

4. Latinos are motivated to please their parents. A building contractor in southern California named Carlos Cardona wanted his daughter to have the musical career he had longed for but never had. "You can be one of the most famous singers in the world," he told her when she was young—and she believed him. For thirty-eight years, she has introduced herself at her performances by her full name, which few in her audience know: Florencia Bicenta de Casillas Martinez Cardona. At eighteen, she was allowed to leave home to take a singing job in Reno at the Holiday Hotel. Soon she was singing on the same bill as Wayne Newton or the Smothers Brothers, now under the stage name of Vikki Carr, working long hours for $200 a week, $170 of which she sent home to her father who couldn't work when the weather was bad.

She made a demo record singing five standards and took it herself to recording companies—where, she was convinced as she sat in the waiting rooms, nobody listened to it before telling her she was "not needed." Finally, someone listened, Liberty Records, and she made a hit with a song called "He's a Rebel"—in Australia. And she recorded "It Must Be Him," only nobody in the U.S. would play it because it contained the lyric "Let it please him, Oh Dear God," and in those days (1966) you couldn't use the Lord's name in a song. You could in England, though, and there she went, where the song became number one in the country. Then the president of Liberty, Al Bennett, saw what she did in England and re-released the song in the States, informing his people, "This time the song will make it, or heads will roll."

Heads didn't. The song reached number one in the United States too, and was followed by such megahits as "Can't Take My Eyes off You" and "With Pen in Hand." Long before Gloria Estefan or Mariah Carey, Vikki Carr was the first Latina to become a star in the general market. Because of her father. Because he let her believe.

5. Latinos are motivated by wanting to do the right thing. When I started my agency, a young man named Ernest Bromley started with me. He was our researcher, and the information he provided enabled me to write ads good enough to let our five-person agency build. Five years later, we had grown to eighteen people and Ernest was making a good salary—$24,000 a year.

One day, somewhat apologetic, he came into my office to announce that the largest advertising agency in San Antonio had offered him a salary of $40,000 if he would come to them.

"Please don't leave," I pleaded.

"I'm sorry," he said, and he genuinely was. "I've already accepted. Look, Lionel, I know you can't afford to match the salary, and besides it would be unfair to the other people here if you did. Wish me luck. We're good friends. Let's keep it at that."

"Okay, good friend," I said, knowing he was right. "We'll announce it to the agency."

I gathered the entire staff together after lunch and made the announcement. The reaction was one of the most amazing I've ever seen. Half the people wept openly. The other half had tears in their eyes. Modest and low-key, Ernest Bromley, a man of innate fairness and total honesty, I realized, was the glue that held the office together. Such people are irreplaceable. That afternoon I offered him a salary of $60,000(!), a new Mercedes, and a new title: Executive Vice President.

He shook his head. "I can't take it," he said. "I've made a commitment."

"But the others," I said. "The people here. They love you and need you. Don't stay for me. Stay for them."

Eventually this argument persuaded him. In a few years Ernest became my partner. Without him—without his chemistry working with all of us—we would not have achieved our degree of success, and my life would be emotionally poorer.

In keeping Ernest with the agency, I broke a number of the rules you'll find in this book. The lesson, of course, is that all rules have exceptions—but there'd better be a compelling reason for the break.

But before I get to the rules—before you can hope to be like Ernest Bromley—I want to describe some people you should *not* emulate: the stereotypes you'll find as you go through your business career.

CHAPTER 3

THE EIGHT LATINO BUSINESS STEREOTYPES

Que no seas uno de ellos

Be careful reading this chapter. Halfway through, you'll be tempted to say, "This is too much! Latinos aren't this bad." But even though there seems to be an overabundance of stereotypes, go ahead and read through it. I think you'll find it helpful in understanding what *not* to do. And from there on the message is positive, I promise.

In some form, you've met them all. If you're in business for yourself, you've dealt with one type or another on a daily basis. If you're part of a firm, you'll probably recognize your boss as one of them. If you're just starting out, you may even find yourself unwittingly emulating a particular type you feel should be admired.

We are what we are because of where we've come from, because of what we've learned, because of what we see around us. Many times I've seen American Latinos fall into these undesirable categories without really understanding why. The roles are easy to adopt and difficult to change, particularly since our culture so often dictates our actions.

Studying the behavior of Anglos won't necessarily help. Many of them fit into these same categories. As Latinos, we seem to slip into them more easily—and have more trouble recognizing them even when they're pointed out.

So watch out: If you find yourself becoming any of the eight types I'm about to describe, *change*!

⟳

I. The *Patrón*

The *patrón*. The boss. The man (or woman) in charge. The supreme commander. Do everything my way, the *patrón* says. Don't do it like that, do it like this. *Hazlo así, no asá*. It's the right way because I say it's the right way. My word is law, my orders are to be obeyed. Don't think for yourself; I'm not paying you to think. I do all the thinking around here.

The *patrón* stereotype cuts across all businesses, smallest to largest. The only thing common to these businesses is that they're not as successful as they could be.

In Latin America, most businesses have one main man (and in 99.9 percent of the cases, it *is* a man). People scurry around him, trying to do his bidding, trying to please him, fearful that any misstep will cost them at best a tongue-lashing, at worst their job.

Mostly, the *patrón* rules through intimidation. The business is his kingdom and he (often subconsciously) feels that fear is the best way to keep his subjects in line.

The best way to handle the *patrón*, his employees feel, is to obey him blindly. If he makes a mistake, one looks the other way or justifies his actions. If his business succeeds, it's because he and he alone made it happen.

Recently I was at a Latino firm in Dallas when, in the course of a meeting, the *patrón* interrupted the discussion to ask a junior executive to pick up his sick child from school; the boy's mother was apparently shopping and couldn't be reached. "And on your way back," the *patrón* added, "pick up my tuxedo at the dry cleaners. There's a formal dinner tonight, and since this meeting's likely to run late, I'll change in the office."

The junior executive sprang from the conference table and

rushed to do his boss's bidding. It was clear he did not resent the order. Indeed, he seemed to look on it as a sign of favor.

If the same incident occurred in an Anglo firm, it most probably would have been accompanied by a "please" (the boss would know he was overstepping his bounds), and few Anglo workers would accept it gladly. But in a Latin American firm, and in most Latino businesses in America, there is simply no such thing as disobedience, and the junior employee asked to do a personal errand for his superior knows that it *is* a sign of favor, and he'll do it willingly every time. *"Como usted mande"*—as you command. Run enough errands, they think, and the boss might find them indispensable. But there would be no thought of a raise or a promotion; a boss's largesse simply doesn't go that far. The Anglo idea of a profit-sharing program is virtually unknown in Latino firms. All profits go to the boss.

Sensing—even *knowing*—that many Anglo business customs such as incentives and empowerment are good for a business, the head of a huge magazine and newspaper distribution company in Mexico City called me in as a consultant. Why, he wondered, was his business not growing? Why, when his was the biggest and most efficient distribution service in a city glutted with periodicals of all kinds (there are twelve daily newspapers, hundreds of popular magazines), did there seem to be a falling away of customers? Why were good workers leaving him for other companies? I was there to give him some American insights.

I liked him immediately. He was open in his questions, honest in his concerns, straightforward in his manner, friendly in his dealings with me and, from what I could see, with his associates.

I asked about the nature of his business. He told me that at three or four each morning his trucks would go to the many newspapers around the city and pick up the daily run, adding magazines when they too came off press. The trucks would bring the publications to a warehouse situated in the city center and, starting at around 5 A.M., the owners of kiosks, candy stores, novelty shops, etc.—most of them small entrepreneurs struggling to eke out an adequate living—would come in to pick up their day's supply of publications and take them back to their places of business, often in carts they would pull themselves.

I suggested to my new friend that he needed to give his business a personality—a "branded" look. Lupe Garcia and I designed a logo for him, and presented a business plan featuring a modest financial incentive program for both his sales staff and the owners of the kiosks and small stores, based on sales goals for the staff and sales results for the owners. Mind you, these were *modest* incentives, far lower than they would be in the United States, meant more as a morale booster than as a real supplement to their very small basic income.

My friend loved the logo and adopted it immediately. But even though he acknowledged that the incentive program might work, he simply couldn't bear the idea of it. *"Esto lo hacemos después"*—we'll do this later. It went against his nature, his training, his culture, his *core*.

Ingrained deep in his subconscious, and dating back to a reaction against the *conquistadores*, was this notion: "Somebody is going to treat me unfairly, somebody is at my back waiting to stick in the knife—so I'd better get all I can while the getting is good." Unfortunately, many people in Mexico feel this way (for good historical reason). So everybody's out to take all they can before they themselves get taken.

This attitude derives as much from master-slave societies of seventeenth-century Latin America as does the attitude of the *peón*, the slave. If you're the boss, you can't be a slave. There is no middle ground.

The *patrón* sees himself as both the *conquistador* (do what I say) and the priest (do what I say because *"así lo quiere Dios"*). Even the most casual student of Latin American politics can see the *patrón* attitude in the leaders of Mexico, Brazil, Venezuela, Argentina, Peru. We'll take what we can, they say by their actions, because it's our time and our time is limited. Understand that American leaders abuse power too; it's heady stuff. Nixon did it. Oliver North did it. Clinton's Whitewater activities suggest an attitude of let's-use-our-power-to-make-the-deals. The difference is that in Latin America, in most cases, that type of activity is almost expected.

Anglo businesspeople can be autocratic, can use fear as a method of control, can be greedy, mean to their employees, pig-headed, egotistical, even corrupt. Indeed, I suspect some of them look at the Latin American *patrón* somewhat wistfully. But overall the majority do not have the same *patrón* approach as their Latino counterparts. I know of none who would turn down a business plan that would increase their personal profits just because it meant sharing some of those profits with the people who work for and with them.

As Latin American business becomes global, as new ideas are introduced from North America and Europe, as dictatorial companies fall behind those attuned to a "quality circle," Latino CEOs will become more "Americanized" in their approach to business. In fact, many have already changed, particularly those educated in the U.S. But it is a difficult transition for many of them, far more difficult in Latin America than it is in this country, for here we are surrounded by companies that empower their people, prospering precisely because they look to others for ideas, trust their employees as colleagues and team members, recognize their own weaknesses and hire people with complementary strengths. For American Latinos to prosper, we will have to do that too. And we will.

You can tell yourself you would never act like a *patrón* and still subconsciously be one. If you find yourself or your boss mouthing or even thinking any of the phrases I'm about to list, watch out. You (or your boss) have an attitude that must be altered in order to succeed.

1. "The only way to get it done right is to do it myself." What you're saying, of course, is that only you are good enough or smart enough; all others around you are inferior. There is only one "right" way, your way. You don't even consider the possibility that there are dozens of other ways. It makes no sense to ask for advice, for who is capable of advising *you?* After all, it's your company!

Well, yes, it *is* your company, but how much better it would be if your people heard "What do you think?" or "How would you handle it?" or "Where do you think we can improve?" or "I don't know about that. Explain it to me." Give your people credit; learn to listen. Then you'll find yourself thinking, "The only way to get it done right is for us to do it together, as a team—*somos un equipo.*" That's the right attitude. The one that succeeds.

2. *"You can't get good help these days—it's impossible to find."* This is simply not true, and if you find yourself thinking it, you're in trouble. Indeed, referring to your employees or team members as "help" is already the wrong attitude, for it implies a boss-servant relationship, not a team-oriented one. You can always find talent when you look for it, and you can always hire good people if you recruit correctly. In fact, you should look for people who are more experienced than you in some areas, people better educated in some aspects of your business, people more seasoned, smarter, more objective, more farsighted. They are out there by the dozens, and they can help make you more successful.

You won't find them if you don't believe they exist. The reality is, they are there and you *will* find them, but first you must really want them. You must want assistance, not assistants. You must believe that you *need* a team, others to share your vision, to help you grow. In fact, that's the *only* way to grow.

3. *"Who's responsible for this mess? ¿Quién la regó?" Patrones* immediately assume that if anything goes wrong, it's someone else's fault. How many times have you heard a manager say the equivalent of "Somebody's got their grubby little mitts on it, and now I've got to clean it up."

But many times foulups come from the boss alone. After all, if the employees are not allowed to disagree and they perform robotically *even when they know there's a better way*, how can they be blamed when something goes wrong? Of course, the *patrón* mentality does not allow the boss to see when someone else's initiative is right. He *assumes* everybody else is wrong—otherwise they'd be *patrones* too—and so what he initiates, like his word, is law.

The head of an architectural firm I know was commissioned to oversee the construction of one of his designs in Tampa. He was inspired by the responsibility and wanted it executed precisely to his specifications, determining to oversee every aspect of the construction personally so nothing would go wrong. The problem was that this approach took three times as long and cost three times more than necessary because he "just had to" make all the decisions himself. For example, the *patrón* wanted a particular color for the inside walls. When he saw them, he said the shade was too light (an associate had specified the color after looking at swatches with him in his office), and he insisted the walls be repainted. The final color was so close to the one already on the wall that nobody else could tell the difference.

Things were built and torn down time after time because he was not there at the precise moment each decision had to be made. Eventually he insisted on seeing everything as it was built, and so the construction workers, who were being paid by the hour, waited for him to arrive before they started work. Finally the building was finished, and since the *patrón* is an expert and has good taste, it is one of the most attractive in Tampa. But the *patrón*'s profits were minimal, and his architectural firm remains about the same size today as it was when the building was finished five years ago.

4. *"These people just don't understand."* The statement implies a master-servant attitude, for what the *patrón* is saying translates to "These people *can't* understand. They're my intellectual inferiors. They're lower than I am because I'm the best." Teamwork is impossible, one person's ego dominates, harmony is shattered, and contributions from people who might very well be the best in the field are simply ignored.

There are other, smaller telltale signs of the *patrón* mentality. As you go through your workday, ask yourself these questions:

- Do you require your assistant to bring you coffee rather than getting it yourself?
- If you're a man, do you tell the women in your office how pretty they look?
- Do you ask your employees to run personal errands for you, such as getting theater tickets, or taking your dog to the vet?
- Do you have a car and driver that you use for personal transportation as well as company business?
- To handle your personal business (taxes, thank-you notes,

etc.), have you hired an assistant who is paid from the company payroll?

- Do you keep all the profits or do you share some portion of them, ten to fifty percent, with your employees in the form of incentive or bonus?
- Do you insist there be no meetings without you present?
- Do you believe that complimenting an employee—"well done"—is beneath you? (After all, the employee is being paid to do a good job.)
- Have you ever criticized an employee in front of others?

Of course, everyone who has ever run a company or worked in a business has been guilty of doing or saying something undesirable. I'm not talking about the occasional "If you're going out to lunch, would you please bring me back a sandwich." I'm talking here about overall attitude. If you see nothing wrong with the above—if you actually *approve*—then the best people will not work for you, corporations will not welcome your participation, you will not grow, you will not succeed, and you will wind up alone, sitting in an empty corner crying over your beer or chardonnay, wondering why, since you are so good, more business isn't coming your way.

2. The *Peón*

Peones, like those in the next two categories (the *Trabajador* and the *Pobrecito*) are the descendants of slaves, not necessarily by birth but by attitude. You'll see immediately how they feed into the power of the *patrón*; indeed, without *peones* and *trabajadores* and *pobrecitos*, the *patrón* could not exist.

A *peón* feels extremely virtuous. He follows orders, has no opinions of his own regarding his boss's wishes, works diligently, rarely if ever complains (and then only to his family), and is always on hand when his superior needs him: after hours, on weekends, in the middle of the night. *Peones* are resigned to taking orders, to assuming the role of the slave. "I will do whatever my *jefe* says," they think, and cannot imagine thinking otherwise.

Unfortunately, millions of Latinos in the United States believe that acting the *péon*—being the *peón*—is the best way to get ahead in life. They will do anything to hold on to their jobs, but they do not see the *peón* role as demeaning, simply as a facet of God's will.

I'm reminded of a talented young copywriter at a competing agency who wanted to please too much. He felt everyone was his *jefe*: the client, the agency owner, the creative director, the senior art director. He tried mightily to satisfy them all—and wound up with ads full of so many different ideas that no one could decipher them.

Again, ask yourself some questions:

- Do you always address your superiors as *señor* or *señora*, using their last names and never their first names?
- When given an order, do you always say, "Yes sir," or "Yes, ma'am, right away"— *"Como usted mande"*?
- Have you ever said, *"Usted solamente moléstese con ordenarme"*? It means "Please take the trouble to order me," and many Latinos now say it as a joke, a self-mockery. But it was once said by *peones* in earnest, and there is too much history embodied in it for me to find it funny.
- Have you ever thought, "My boss is wrong," but followed his order anyway, without giving serious consideration to expressing your opinion?
- Have you ever been pleased to do a personal errand for your boss?
- Have you ever worked overtime on a seemingly trivial task, and been happy you were given the work to do?
- Are you content with the basics: security, no responsibility, adequate shelter, simple but plentiful food, a good spouse and obedient children? (All of which are fine, but I suggest that if you're reading this book you want more out of life.)
- Perhaps most important, do you uncomplainingly follow orders at work but see yourself as a *patrón* at home, where your word and your word alone is a command? (This is a common side result of the *peón* mentality; after all, frustration must be taken out somewhere.)

Patently, there is nothing wrong with following orders, with working hard, with doing the best you can for a boss—or a client (for bosses, as we'll see, can be *peones*, too)—even if he does not reward you. It's *mind-set* I'm concerned with here, a mind-set that must be changed if you want to compete and succeed.

The first step toward change, as for all categories, is to recognize and acknowledge your attitude. Then, try an experiment. Pick a moment to express your own opinion, whether by saying "no" to weekend work, or by suggesting a different way to do a job, or by introducing an innovation. You may get a variety of responses: amusement, astonishment, condescension, anger, appreciation. But you will not get fired, nor will you lose your client. When your stomach settles down (for confrontation, disobedience, and aggressiveness are never easy) you find that your world hasn't exploded. In fact, you'll have gained a measure of self-confidence that will make the next difference of opinion with your boss or client easier and the next suggestion less daunting to offer.

And you will begin to move forward in the business world. And up.

3. The *Trabajador*

The Anglos have an expression, "An honest day's work for an honest day's pay," and this is what the *trabajador* lives by. Descendants of an agrarian tradition, often working in manual trades like farming, construction, garment manufacturing (even if it's in the sweatshops of New York or South America) or as gardeners, waiters, maids, nannies, *trabajadores* believe in sweat. Indeed, the more they sweat and the harder they work, the more virtuous they feel. *"Hay que trabajar duro, el trabajo es honor."* They attach lesser importance to wit, intellect, education. If you work long and hard in *any* job, as long as it's honest work, they're convinced, you're on the right path. Where? That's hard to say. But no matter. Money, the ability to provide, is the goal for the *trabajador*, and the way to earn it is by the strength of your back.

These are the questions to ask yourself to find out if you have a *trabajador* mentality:

- Have you said to your children, "What are you doing in school? Go to work. We need you to start earning money."
- Have you ever told your compatriots or employees, "Work as hard as I do. It feels great! Last week I put in a hundred hours."
- Have you boasted, "I get up at dawn. I'm always the first one at work, the last one to leave."
- As soon as you finish one job, do you start on the next?
- "As long as you work hard, everything will be all right." Is this your philosophy? Do you try to instill it in your children?

Believe me, I have nothing against hard work; there's a lot of the *trabajador* in my makeup. My Anglo friends describe me as a workaholic. My wife (who works hard herself) is constantly urging me to slow down. I am financially secure, but I would be miserable if I didn't work. I love it!

Still, work is not all there is to life. To work without play, to work solely to make money for security *without recognizing that work must be accompanied by a balanced goal, a life plan,* is an ultimately self-defeating process. Working hard is an essential for success. But it must be accompanied by education, by a philosophy of life, and by periods of rest and contemplation.

The Anglos have another expression: "All work and no play makes Jack a dull boy." I would add, "Makes Jack a *pendejo*."

4. The *Pobrecito*

Even if we aren't *pobrecitos* ourselves, we all know them: the prophets of doom, the perpetual victims, the entrepreneurs whose businesses, and lives, somehow always seem not to meet expectations, their own expectations, except when they expect to fail.

Pobrecitos go into business without having thought their business through. They have no long-term plans (why have them if failure is inevitable?), don't or can't think big, don't want to expand (on that path disaster surely lies), think only of the short term (whew! another day gone and nothing terrible has happened). Like *peones*, they can be the heads of their own businesses, but whereas the *peón* will treat his clients with a smiling servility that will chase many away, the *pobrecito* will do it with frowns. He considers ambition futile, experimentation dangerous, a plan for the future a recipe for bankruptcy.

Here's how the *pobrecito* thinks:

"I'll work myself to the bone but I still won't be able to find real success."

"Life is a continual sacrifice."

"Business is tough, and it never seems to get better."

"I'd better not reinvest in the business. It's like throwing money away."

"I know things look good now, but they won't stay that way."

"There'll be a recession."

"There'll be a depression."

"It's the competition."

"It's the economy."

5. The *Aventurero*

"Go for it," *aventureros* think, a lot like an Anglo. But they go without planning ahead, without analyzing, without researching. They're always looking for a new and better business, a new and better way. To an *aventurero* preplanning is a waste of time, a market study just squanders money better spent on office space, a five-year plan is a meaningless dream. Dream *now*, the *aventurero* seems to be saying. Something good will happen. And hey! If not this time, the next. All I can say is, I like to have an *aventurero* across the table from me in a poker game.

My brother Dan, even though he's over fifty and should know better, is an *aventurero*. I love him dearly. He always asks for brotherly advice, then does his own thing anyway, different from the advice. He's always looking for a new way to make a buck. Recently he decided to become a greengrocer, and bought a small building on a major thoroughfare lined with auto repair and chrome shops. The building was cheap and, as he explained to me when he approached me for advice about his plan, "Think of all that traffic!"

"But why would cars *stop*?" I asked him.

"Because everybody likes fresh vegetables."

"What'll attract them?"

"The sight of fresh fruits. Everybody likes color."

"At fifty-five miles an hour? Isn't there a supermarket less than a quarter mile away?"

"Sure, but who likes to shop in supermarkets?"

I do, I thought, particularly when I can do one-stop shopping there. But I did not say this to Dan, for it was obvious he was going to start his business despite my opinion. I simply advised him that, to my way of thinking, it would be tough to make it really successful, and as I suspected, he went ahead anyway.

As it turned out, on a good day he'd take in twenty dollars, more often six or twelve. Much of the produce spoiled. And he had to sell what remained at a noncompetitive price.

Soon the grocery became a flea market. Then, when that failed, he leased the building to a church and his wife persuaded him to take a job as a salesman. Dan is one of the most delightful people I know, with a great smile and a wonderful style. His wife had found him an outlet for his true talent. But he was ever the *aventurero*. Last time we visited, Dan told me he's studying to be a personal-injury attorney. "That's where the money is," he says.

"I know I can do it," the *aventurero* thinks. "*Lo siento en el corazón.*"

"I don't need to do the figures. I just *know* it's right."

"This can't miss!"

"The children need it. I'm doing it for them."

"The family needs it. I'm doing it for them."

"The community needs it. I'm doing it for them."

"This is an ideal spot for a business. Look at all that traffic."

6. The *Romántico*

The *romántico* and the *aventurero* have much in common. They are both dreamers, both unrealistic, but the *romántico* is sensitive: the artist, the poet, the songwriter, the performer. *Románticos* work from the heart, not the head. They're convinced of their talent, need only a hearing (a reading, a viewing, an audition) to prove how good they are. They'll succeed once the world becomes aware of their talent.

Some of them, of course, *are* talented, some of them *do* succeed, but even the successful ones need business managers and financial advisors; their hearts as well as their heads are someplace else.

Most don't take the fundamental first steps. I've had candidates for jobs approach me with messy or incomplete portfolios. An advertising executive described a copywriter who expected to land a well-paying job on the basis of his personality. He believed his ideas were so good, his enthusiasm so infectious, he didn't have to bother to bring sample ads he'd written. Songwriters, artists, performers—even copywriters—who cannot accept the fact that maybe they're just not talented *enough*, waste their lives dreaming of the "big hit" or the "ideal job." Many have no business acumen, and allow what talent they have to be exploited.

I like *románticos*. My own dream of becoming another Picasso has not died, it's just been put aside. Creative talent is a wondrous thing, but often it should be developed while you have a steady job.

"I have a gift from God," the *romántico* says. "It would be an injustice if I did not share it with the world."

"I was born to sing."

"I'd rather starve than work in a company."

"All businesspeople are evil."

"I'll never sell out!"

"Billionaire Emilio Ezcarraga was just lucky—or maybe he deals in drugs."

"I don't need an agent."

"Take a writing course? The true artist doesn't need to learn technique."

"If Gloria Estefan can do it, so can I."

"I'm as talented as Diego Rivera."

"I trust my gut. What I've composed is *good.*"

The *aventurero* and the *romántico* are also formed by their master-slave heritage and are running from it, often in subconscious fear. Their past isn't going to trap *them*, they vow. They'll do anything to avoid it—anything except accept reality.

7. The *Soy un Minority*

Of all the types, the *soy un minority* is the saddest. Such people feel the world owes them something simply because they were born Hispanic. If there are two candidates for a job, they think the Latino should win just because of the "prejudice" it would demonstrate if the Anglo were chosen. Even if the Anglo is better qualified, has prepared a more thought-through presentation, or simply made a better impression at the job interview, it would not be "fair" for the Anglo to get the job. In other words, they believe in a kind of reverse racism that does little to enhance the Latino role in America, that indeed perpetuates the stereotype, thus holding back other striving Latinos who believe in winning on skill.

They rely on government set-aside grants and fume when the grants run out ("See, we were right all along—without the grants we'd never have gotten the job") even though most do nothing to wean themselves and their businesses from the government teat.

These Latinos deny their slave mentality, but it leaks out of them. They use their ancestors' serfdom as a crutch, as an excuse, as *the* reason for personal reward.

"I'm going to take the short cut," they seem to say. "Why do all that extra stuff when I'm owed the job anyway?"

"Why should I compete for a job? Sooner or later the grant will come through and I'll get the job without effort. Then I'll be set."

There are other attitudes the *soy un minority* holds:

"All Anglos are prejudiced. Even if I'm more qualified I won't get the job."

"I'd never work in an Anglo firm. There's no opportunity for Hispanics."

"Those more fortunate owe me something."

"It may be that all men are created equal, but some are more equal than others, and I'm not one of them."

8. The *Sonso*

Again, their past molds them. *Sonsos* are the people too afraid to compete, too vulnerable to go far from where they were born, comfortable only among their "own kind," relaxed with other *sonsos* who reaffirm the value of safety over opportunity.

They often work hard, and they're often intelligent, but they *act* dumb because that way no one can ask them for aggressiveness, innovation, gumption. The idea of researching an opportunity, or sending their children away to college, is anathema. After a failure, even if they've been partly responsible, they plead ignorance. "But I didn't know" is their catchphrase, "it's not my fault" their refrain.

Here's what the *sonso* is likely to think:

"Don't blame me."

"A chance for a good job in New York? I'm content here in Cotula."

"You can learn as much at our community college as you can at Harvard or any other of the snobby schools."

"In the old country, life was simple. Sometimes I wish my parents had never left to come here."

"I'm satisfied with what I've got."

"When your boss comes looking, *desaparécete*—disappear."

"When opportunity knocks, don't answer the door."

↜

Recognize yourself in any of these types? Of course. We are all human, and each of us has felt powerful, powerless, assertive, shy, hesitant, ambitious, lazy, hard-working, timid, self-important, defensive, worthless, small, and large at one time or another in our lives. But if you feel you fall *primarily* into one of the types described above—if you *are* a *patrón* or a *trabajador* and not just sometimes *patrón*-like or *trabajador*-like—then you should try to change.

How do you rid yourself of these attitudes?

- Examine yourself closely and honestly to see if you indeed fall into one of these types. Ask your family (sometimes difficult to do), your coworkers, your friends. You may be surprised how insightful and helpful they can be if you ask in earnest and are receptive, not defensive, when they open up.
- Train consciously to be the opposite. Catch yourself when you fall into a pattern.
- Study the behavior of others to pick up what you yourself are doing or not doing.
- Internalize your training so you can *blend* attributes, choosing the right one for the appropriate situation. The more you know different personality types, the better you can adjust to situations and the more tolerant you'll be of the differences in people.
- Believe in yourself and in humanity. You are not so different from everybody else. No one has a patent on goodness, on power, on self-worth. Most colleagues know that as you grow stronger and more confident, so will they, and that as you become more willing to work with others, they can work better with and for you.
- Try not to emulate any of the types described here. Go on to the next chapter, where I discuss the characteristics of *successful* Latino businesspersons, and do your best to emulate them.

CHAPTER 4

THE TWELVE TRAITS OF SUCCESSFUL LATINOS

Puedes ser como ellos

When I first thought of *The Americano Dream,* this chapter was the one I most wanted to write. I have spent some forty years in business, and during that time I have met innumerable successful businesspersons, all of whom shared some or most of the traits I'll describe in this chapter. I've tried to understand and adopt as many of these traits as I could in my own life. To be maximally successful, you must adopt them too. If you do, my book will have served its primary purpose.

The traits of success are shared, of course, by both Anglos and Latinos. However, Anglos are more relentless in their pursuit of success. *They,* not we, developed the American ethic of over-achievement above everything else. It is their creation. If we want to play, *we* must adapt. We must want to be *número uno.* The Anglo has a beat-the-competition, winning-is-everything, first-is-the-only-place-to-finish approach to business life. That's not our nature. As already noted, the difference lies in the fact that we were conditioned as underachievers. We, the descendants of slaves and conquerors, have a survival approach to business. In America, that's not good enough. You have to make a decision to compete or not to compete. If you *do* want to compete, read on.

I. Successful Latinos Know What They Want, Believe in Their Ability to Get It, and Believe They Deserve Success

Everything starts with believing you deserve to succeed. Then you must set a goal. To attain your goals you must first believe that achieving them is possible. You must believe this reality with so much passion that nothing will deter you. Your goals must be much more specific than "I want financial independence" or "I want happiness." These are things everybody wants, but they're so general as to be virtually meaningless. Make your goals clear, specific, definite—unique to you, coming out of *your* life's passion and wildest desires, goals with a firm time limit ("I will achieve Y in X years"), goals that once achieved will lead to additional goals in the years ahead.

The goals need not be monetary—*"El dinero no es todo"*—they can be goals that improve others' lives; they can be goals for yourself; they can be goals for your children or friends or community. You may not always be able to see the road that leads to your goal at first. But soon it appears, as if someone magically constructed it for you. Once known, the road to success will take many unexpected twists and turns before you reach your destination, but if the goal remains constant, it will be the beacon that keeps you on course.

My first goal in business was to make enough money through my artistic ability to support my family; my second was to create the largest design firm in South Texas; my third was to build the largest Hispanic advertising agency in San Antonio; my fourth was to make it the largest in the United States. I achieved each of these goals in the allotted time frame. My current one, still in the setting-up stage, is the establishment of the first multiethnic agency in America that specifically targets Latinos, Asians, and African-Americans.

In each case, I gave myself five years to achieve the goal, then devoted the next little while to mapping out a new goal. Five seems the right number to me, but you may want to give yourself lesser or greater time limits. The time span must be long enough to ensure that the goal is "big," but not so long that reaching it seems an eternity away. A vacation for next summer or a new wardrobe are good goals, but not the Big Goals I'm describing— not the kind that form the "beacon."

When I talk about goals with successful people, they all agree that they had a specific goal clearly in mind long before they reached the positions they hold today.

- Henry Cisneros, Secretary of Housing and Urban Development in the first Clinton administration, had a burning desire to be the best public servant in American politics before he was forty-five.
- The novelist and poet Sandra Cisneros (no relation to Henry) determined to have her first work published by the time she graduated from college, then wanted to be the best-known Latino writer in the United States.
- Johnny Gabriel, now one of San Antonio's most generous individuals and most successful businesspeople, has had, together with his wife Rosalee, several goals: to build his own business to preeminence, to help young people get educated, and to conduct himself with complete integrity so he brings honor to his family, to his children, and to the Gabriel name.
- Al Aguilar, my former partner, wanted to be at the top of the Hispanic advertising field by the time he was forty. Al is fiercely proud of his Latino culture and heritage. To him, the thought that Latinos in advertising should be treated differently from anyone else, or the merest hint that Latino ad budgets should be smaller than Anglos', reeks of unfairness. (*"¡Un Latino vale lo mismo que un gringo!"*) He once got a $930,000 budget from Coca-Cola to film Latinos drinking Coke in New York, Texas, Florida, and California. He argued that four separate crews for the location shots were needed to ensure authenticity, and Coke agreed. The result was considered the most beautiful and effective ad ever made for a Latino audience. For the Bromley Aguilar agency, it remains a source of tremendous pride. For Al, it was all in a day's work.

- My favorite example of a goal realized revolves around Lou Agnese. Lou is an Italian from Brooklyn, but he's lived so long in the Southwest that he claims to be more Latino than the Latinos. His story illustrates exactly what this chapter is about.

Lou had just been hired as president of Incarnate Word College in San Antonio. It was a small school, and like many private colleges in 1986 it had slowly been losing enrollment for eight years straight. Lou made it his goal to turn the downward trend around. He believed with all his heart that he could do it, and he knew that advertising was the key. All he needed was a million-dollar ad campaign, and students would come flocking!

Of course, he didn't *have* a million dollars—he had none. But he had a goal and an idea. He came to me for help.

"Let's trade media time for scholarships," he said. "A television station gives me a quarter of a million dollars' worth of airtime, they get a quarter of a mil worth of scholarships. I want you to help me approach the stations."

"It's a lousy idea, Lou," I said. "*¡Estás bien loco!* What would a television station do with all those scholarships?"

"Give them to deserving, needy students. What does anybody do with scholarships?"

"Where would they find the students?"

He smiled. "They wouldn't. I would. That's the beauty of it. They'd get the glory, the good publicity, and I'd get the kids."

I wasn't convinced and told him so.

"Hey," Lou said, "I did it in Sioux City. The media loved it and I doubled the enrollment of the college I was running."

I was astonished. "It worked in Sioux City?"

"Yup."

"Okay." I sighed. "I'll help you."

It worked in San Antonio. In five years, enrollment doubled; in ten, it tripled. For his achievements Lou was invited to meet the president at the White House. Later, as we congratulated each other on Lou's success, he made a confession. "I never did it in Sioux City. But I needed you to believe. So I told a white lie. You believed it, and we saved the college."

I don't advocate lying (though what he did doesn't seem so terrible), but I do admire Lou's gumption, his single-mindedness, his specificity. He knew exactly what his timeline was. He knew exactly how much he wanted to increase enrollment, and he achieved it. At the time, it seemed unreachable to me. But to him, it was totally realistic. That's why he achieved it.

If you knew these people, you'd realize that all of them set goals in spheres where they had shown talent early on, that their goals were hard won and came from an inner passion, a fire that drove them through adversity to success.

As noted, it's not enough to say, "I want to be happy—*quiero ser feliz*" or "I want to be healthy—*quiero tener buena salud*" or "I hope my children will grow up better than me."

Here are some examples of my specific goals; make up a similar list for yourself.

- "I will build the largest Hispanic advertising agency in the United States by year's end 1995."
- "I will transfer management to my partners, assuring a lifetime income for me and security for my family."
- "Next year I will be healthier and stronger than the year before. I will get regular checkups every twelve months. I will improve my strength, flexibility, and cardiovascular endurance. I will eat no more than thirty grams of fat a day, will drink in moderation, and will meditate to decrease stress."
- "I will participate in my children's school activities, encouraging them every step of the way. I won't criticize them. I will love them and give them a sense of self. I will give them roots."

If the goal is realistic, you will achieve it. Follow the beacon. Its light shines true.

2. Successful Latinos Are Not "Professional Hispanics"

Here we have the antithesis of the *soy un minority*. These are men and women who take an active *pride* in being Latino, who use their lineage not as an excuse or a crutch but as a source of inspiration. There is a huge difference between wanting to be, say, the best-known Latino writer and being a writer who feels she deserves to be published merely because she is Latino. Henry Cisneros indeed used his Latino-ness as a springboard for his political rise, but it became obvious to the president that no one was better qualified, whatever his race. It was a bonus that Henry was also able in the cabinet to represent ten percent of the U.S. population. Roberto Goizueta, chairman of Coca-Cola, did not rely on minority set-asides. He relied on those aspects of the Latino character that came naturally to him—hard work, loyalty, honesty, a devotion to family, civic-mindedness. These traits were part of his heritage and would persuade his management to promote him. Once promoted, he proved himself able—the *most* able—and so rose to the top.

Successful Latinos don't have an ethnic chip on their shoulders. They don't need "entitlements." They don't whine about prejudice—*"pobre de mí"*—and minority participation (although they are not blind to prejudice and fight hard for a Latino presence in the business world), and they don't think they'll succeed or fail because of their ethnicity.

These Latinos succeed because they are willing and able to compete in the real world, albeit an Anglo world. Their position is achieved through inner confidence and strength, not ceded them by the government or a corporation having to fill a moral "minority quota." They may indeed aim to be the best in their field. They know who they are and where they come from. They want their success to be a motivation for other Latinos; they want to set an example.

3. Successful Latinos Don't Carry the Weight of the World on Their Shoulders

They have shed the ghosts of their past, though not its glories. If they have an accent, they speak up with pride and class! If their skin is dark, they wear it with honor. They dwell not on slights or rejections but on possibilities. Prejudice, they believe, is not rele-

vant to their own situation. If they encounter it, they pity the pur-
veyor, not themselves. "Poor ignorant soul," said a buddy of mine
when we were called "spics" by our drill sergeant in boot camp.
The racial slur did not get him down; in fact, he worked harder
than ever and graduated with honors. Richly aware of their heritage, successful Latinos know that when the roots run deep, so
does the pride.

An essential element for Latino success is the knowledge that,
when the cultural luggage we carry is heavy, we must discard the
negative part, keeping only the positive, in order to move faster
and rise higher. Once we are free of it we are free to achieve our
goals, to be confident of the future and confident of ourselves.

4. Successful Latinos Are Optimists

Mateo and Angela Garcia arrived here penniless from Cuba
some thirty years ago. He was able to start a small used-furniture
business, though they had to scratch for a living. She took care of
the home in the traditional Latina fashion. Together they poured
their love and dreams into their children, Elizabeth and Felicita.

He was a natural optimist, she a natural pessimist (opposites *do*
attract). When it came time for Elizabeth to go to college, Angela
argued that their girl should stay close to home. *"Que Dios no lo
quiera,"* she said. "She'll be hurt in a hostile world. Besides, she
can learn as much at a community college as she would at those
faraway fancy universities with nothing but rich snobby students."
But Mateo insisted she should accept the scholarship she was
awarded by a school three thousand miles away.

Mateo got his way, and Elizabeth went to Stanford, then on to
Yale Law School. She became a fine mergers and acquisitions
lawyer, earning $500,000 a year, and one Christmas she surprised
her parents with a tremendous gift: a new house not far from Miami Beach.

Angela was horrified. To her, it wasn't right. "We didn't *earn*
this house," she wailed. "We can't accept it. I don't want to profit
from somebody else's success, even my daughter's."

"Of course we earned it," Mateo said. "We brought her up.

Now she's shown how proud she is of the way we did it. Of course we earned the house. Her success is *our* success."

To me, the story represents the basic difference between optimism and pessimism. The two parents shared the same story, lived the same life, but their outlooks were entirely different. One was positive, the other negative. When their younger daughter, Felicita, quit college to start her own business, it was a tragedy to Angela, an opportunity to Mateo. "It means she has an independent spirit," he said. "She's on her own, doing what she loves. She'll be just as successful as Elizabeth, you wait and see." Sure enough, this child is now a high-ranking executive in the entertainment business. "*Te lo dije*—I told you so," Mateo says.

Attitude influences end results. Remember Lou Agnese? His optimism has continued long after his goal was fulfilled. Incarnate Word is now a university, and Lou has turned part of the vastly enlarged campus into an international meeting and educational center. His fledgling facility is now widely recognized. In fact, *Business Week* ranked it number one nationally in its category.

A recent study reported in *Psychology Today* suggests that optimism is part of our genetic structure, preset at birth. People who are born with it carry it with them through school ("I've failed this test, but I'll ace the next one"), through relationships ("That's the spouse for me; we'll have a happy marriage"), through adversity ("We lost today, but we'll win tomorrow"), even through old age ("The older I get the wiser I am"). No matter what happens, they look on the bright side; for them, always, the glass is half full, not half empty.

But I'm not convinced that the only way you can be an optimist is to inherit the characteristic. It can be learned—in fact, *must* be learned, if we are to succeed. Of all the traits listed in this chapter, to me it is the most important, for without it you cannot begin to plan, you cannot present a positive attitude in a meeting or interview, you cannot attract clients or compete for business, and it becomes difficult to rebound from failure.

At first, we must literally *force* ourselves into an optimistic mind-set, practicing optimism as we would a golf swing or a foreign language. It may be awkward at first, but optimism can become fluid and fluent, so natural to us we no longer think about it. It becomes part of our bloodstream.

We met a kind of optimist in the last chapter: the *aventurero*. But I'm talking here of optimism grounded in reality, not dreams. True optimists look at the situation and react positively to what they see, good or bad. Success in life is the proof of the optimistic personality—in school, career, relationships, personal life.

Pessimists will talk about what's not right in life (*"Nunca puedo avanzar"*—I just can't ever get ahead), about how badly they were treated by others, about the unevenness of the playing field, about the coming recession, the inevitability of war, the spread of disease. They gloat over the misfortunes of others. If a client becomes unhappy with them, they'll look for another client, certain they're about to lose the business anyway.

Optimists believe the world is basically fair, that humanity is mostly beneficent, that they have as good a chance as anybody, that the economy is good for them and will even improve. Diplomacy can avert armed conflict, a cure will be found for the disease. They rejoice in the successes of others. If a client is angry with them, they will take the opportunity to talk it out, redouble their efforts on his behalf, and use the increased dialogue to bond. They believe they'll not only keep the client but increase the business they do with him.

Herb Kelleher, CEO of Southwest Airlines, warns against hiring anybody who complains of being badly treated by his or her previous employer. "Our applicants must have a sense of humor," he counsels. "They must have a positive attitude, a problem-solving attitude. The technical stuff you can teach them; the right attitude you can't. So that's what you should look for."

5. Successful Latinos Trust Others

This is the most controversial trait, the one most disputed by my friends when I discuss it with them. Most of them say, "No, man! Before you trust anyone, study them, check them out!"—like the background checks the government often conducts on potential employees. "Some people can be trusted, others not," they say, "and how do you know which is which? It's better to be wary than sorry."

On the surface, this appears to be a sound, sensible approach, but ultimately it is self-defeating. Overcaution and lack of trust breed more caution and more lack of trust, to the point that everyone is distrustful. I believe that 99.9 percent of all people want to be trustworthy and honest. If you yourself are trustworthy and honest they will respond in kind. Thinking the worst means getting the worst. The time spent on suspicion is better spent on forward-looking enterprise. I'm not saying you shouldn't read a contract carefully before you sign it, or ask for recommendations before hiring someone. But if you assume you can trust, you *can* trust! We're looking here at *mind-set.* You're reading the contract more for fairness and accuracy than with the sense that someone is out to get you; you're asking for references to round out your knowledge of the person, or simply as a confirmation of your own favorable impression.

I developed my trusting attitude early in my business career. We had just opened a design studio in a ground-floor office at the corner of Brooklyn and St. Mary's Streets in San Antonio. Directly above us was a photographer, and he and I became good friends. When he invited me up for coffee one morning, I noticed a curious phenomenon. His front door was triple-protected with a regular lock, a padlock, and a deadbolt. Each drawer of his desk had its own padlock. His telephone was in one of the drawers, also locked, presumably to prevent someone—maybe from *our* office—from sneaking up to make long distance calls when he was out. Often when he was in his darkroom and the phone rang, by the time he could get to his desk and unlock the drawer to try to answer it, it had stopped ringing. To him, it was "just being careful—*precaucioso.*" Losing some business, he explained, was part of the price he paid to be protected.

Actually, though, his office was robbed three times in a year, while ours—more accessible, often unlocked, and with equally valuable equipment—remained untouched. He spent almost as much time on insurance claims as on photography. He eventually got out of the business because, he told me, he did not want to have to guard valuable equipment. He's a repairman now, carefully watching his tools, I'm sure. Meanwhile our agency flourished. This story means simply that trust breeds trust, distrust breeds distrust.

I've known bosses who mistrust their employees, sure that unless the workers are carefully monitored they'll steal or goof off. And I've known other bosses who trust their employees totally, feeling that collegiality, a common goal, *and trust* are the surest ways to get peak performance. In every case, the trusting boss is more successful. Good atmosphere produces good work; trust engenders loyalty. We wind up getting what we expect. If we trust, we tend to expect the best, and the best is our reward.

6. Successful Latinos Are Flexible

Life changes—*"Todo en la vida cambia."* The unexpected happens; things unforeseeable and uncontrollable crop up in everyone's business life. The good entrepreneur can be momentarily unbalanced by sudden misfortune or failure, but *momentarily* is the operative word. No business plan should be so rigid that it does not take fluctuation into account. Successful businesspeople must be prepared to change if circumstances demand it, to rebound if adversity befalls.

Optimism is the cornerstone of flexibility, and the ability to respond rapidly to changing situations is a key to business success. A client suddenly cuts his order in half? Don't panic. Call first to find out all you can about what's going on. Use it as an opportunity to bond. Quote new prices, a new schedule. Who knows? If you service him through a tough time, the order might double the next time around.

Another example: The price of goods has gone up by five percent since the contract was signed. Don't fret. Stick with the original bid, eat the loss this time. The client will give you his business from now on.

Or say the "sure" job suddenly disappears. Don't despair. Another will arrive.

When my agency was young, our largest account by far was the U.S. Army. We were subcontractors to the general market agency,

N. W. Ayer, with the responsibility of "selling" the army to the Hispanic market. The army accounted for fifty percent of our business and we were servicing them creatively and performing to a very high standard. But all was not well. Ayer informed us one black Monday that the army had fired them—which meant that we too were fired. I went directly to the army in an effort to keep the business as subcontractor to their new general market agency, but they turned me down because their new agency already had a Hispanic division.

We had to retrench, and the solution was to cut our staff of sixteen in half. I met with my partners, and grimly we made up the list of names. A few were easy—the ones we felt were not critical. The key positions were more difficult, so we decided to do it by seniority; the newest employees would be cut, the rest kept.

Becky Arreaga, an account executive, was one of the newest, but letting her go was difficult, since at age twenty-three she had already proved herself bright, diligent, capable, creative. Still, we could not keep her; it would have been unfair to the others.

I went into her office, explained the circumstances, handed her a severance check, and assured her that she would be the first to be rehired when we replaced the business and that she would also have my highest recommendation when she applied for a new position. She understood, thanked me, and continued with her work.

The next morning I arrived at work expecting to see eight employees. There were nine! Becky was at her desk, exactly as though nothing had happened.

"What are you doing here?" I asked. "I can't pay you."

"I know," she said calmly. "But this is a good firm, *aquí estoy bien,* and I'd rather work here than anywhere else. I can afford not to be paid for a little while. We'll get new business, and when we do you can pay me again. In fact, you'll probably give me a raise."

I was stunned. She had adapted to our new circumstance with far more optimism than I, a man who thought of himself as the model optimist, the model goal-setter. And she was right. In three weeks we had won the Domino's Pizza account and we hired her again—with a raise. She became one of the top executives at Sosa,

Bromley, Aguilar, Noble and Associates. Now she's in business for herself, doing better than ever.

7. Successful Latinos Visualize Success

If you have a clear goal, one of the ways to make sure you reach it is to visualize exactly what your life will look like when you get there—how you will look physically and what you will be surrounded by. It is as though you make a drawing in your brain, filling in all the details: color, shape, texture.

I learned the technique about the time Leonard Dyke was telling me that thousands of people all around me made more than forty dollars a week. I had been hired to design a sign for a new business school, an extension course of Napoleon Hill's Science of Personal Achievement. After learning what they offered, I decided to attend the classes myself. They were taught not by the great Hill himself but by a woman named Sally Pond. If Hill was more inspirational than she, he could make mountains walk.

Some people, she said, can visualize naturally. They can see themselves, their family, their possessions in the future. But most have to learn it, train for it, work at it. She asked the class to think five or ten years ahead (the time doesn't make much difference but, like the setting of goals, it must be conceivable).

Sit down by yourself, *a solas,* in a quiet, isolated place. You can turn on soothing music, but no television, no radio, no phone. Shut your eyes. If you're thirty, imagine yourself at forty. And then visualize the *entire* day. Begin in the morning. Who is next to you in bed when you wake up? What does your bedroom look like, the size of the bed, the rug, the furniture, the pictures on the wall? Now, in your mind, get up. Go to the bathroom. What does your face look like? Has your hair changed color? Are there lines around your eyes? Mentally walk down your hallway. Are there other bedrooms off it? Children within them? What does your kitchen look like and what are you having for breakfast? Do you drive to work? If so, what color and make of car? What does your office look like? Are you the boss, an executive, a regular worker?

Continue your visualization until it takes you through the whole day, perhaps through making love and falling asleep at night after dinner out and an evening of theater. The point is that this is *your* visualization; it will teach you what you want, what your realistic dreams are, what you should aim for. The whole process should take about an hour. (I recommend doing it just before you go to bed at night, but any time will do as long as you do it regularly and uninterrupted.)

You may find it difficult at first, perhaps even "stupid," a waste of time. But I assure you it is neither. Do it twice a week, and within a few weeks it will become routine, and it will sharpen your brain, make your goals concrete, give you something to look forward to, bring you inspiration when things are going badly and joy when things are going well. The more you do it, the clearer your future will become and the more apt it is to turn out as you wish. Believe me. I do it still.

8. Successful Latinos Overachieve Consistently— *Con Gusto*

Doing more than you're paid to do is an art—an art of attitude, of performance, of outlook. A common expression is "service with a smile," but I'm talking about much more than smiling. If you deliver a promised job a day before it's due; if you provide three plans when you've contracted for two; if you add a flourish, throw in a surprise gift, knock yourself out to deliver more than what's expected, *and you do it with grace, with pleasure, with pride,* I guarantee you your business will thrive. You'll keep and grow the customers or clients you already have, perhaps the most important aspect of successful growth in business.

For years my former agency worked with a television commercial production company called Match Frame. At KJS, we give them our business as well. For them, no task is too big, no request too outrageous, no chore too onerous. They treat us as if we're their only customer (though they have dozens). Their owners, Don White, Ken Ashe, and Mike Bowie, and their representatives, are on call for us nights and weekends and holidays, for emergencies, whenever the unexpected crisis occurs.

They're not the cheapest production company around, but they are reasonable and their work is invariably first-rate. They're always on time and on budget—and they do more than we expect *con gusto*. Often they will suggest production techniques and slight changes that will save us money. They invest in new equipment consistently, which has improved the quality of our television commercials. And always they're friendly, innovative, and open to suggestions. As a result, we won't change companies, no matter what their competition might offer. *No hay una buena razón*—there's no reason to do it.

It's easy to do more, to add grace notes, to provide the niceties that will make you stand out. After a while it becomes a habit. All it takes is imagination and enthusiasm. If you love what you're doing, you'll do it easily. Your clients will love you. And they'll never leave you.

9. Successful Latinos Always Do What They Say They'll Do

There is a motto put up in the office of the San Francisco Superintendent of Schools that reads DWYSYWD. Everybody knows what it means, backwards or forwards: "Do what you say you will do." (Or, in Spanish, *Dicho y hecho:* Once spoken, it's done.)

Good advice. Even if you can't overdeliver—and obviously there will be times when overdelivering is impossible—make sure that you fulfill your contract, your assignment, your promise.

This is going to sound stereotypical, but to a very large degree it is our Latino nature to promise and then to feel okay if we don't quite meet that promise. Partly it's a reluctance to say an initial "no" and partly it's a *"costumbre,"* a custom in our mother countries. "Let's have dinner next Wednesday at eight," one businessman says to another. "Great," the other says. Both know that the arrangement is tenuous at best; they may meet at nine-thirty or not have dinner at all, depending on the circumstances under which the date was made. Despite its specificity, it's nothing more than an exchange of pleasantries, like the Anglo's vague "let's do lunch sometime."

In their home countries, Latinos are often late for business meetings. When I, American born and American trained, went to my first 9 A.M. meeting in Mexico City, I arrived ten minutes early, and the man I was meeting swept in forty-five minutes late, smiling and without apology. I was furious (an Anglo colleague had advised me to leave any meeting where the other person was more than twenty minutes late). Is he *flojo*, I thought, or *loco*? Lazy or crazy? Maybe he's merely inconsiderate. I knew some Anglos who used lateness as a kind of power trip, but they were rare—and generally unsuccessful. When I understood that my compatriot was simply "in Rome, doing what Romans do," my anger subsided, but I vowed that once back in the States I would be even more careful. Not only to be on time, but to make sure that I kept every business promise I made: delivery dates, specifications, costs. *Dicho y hecho.*

I knew enough not to overpromise. It's far better simply to say "I can't" than to try to find out you can't after you've said you could. More firms have lost customers through promises unfulfilled than for any other reason. A reputation as a person of your word is the most important you can have.

Now comes *"lo confeso"*—I confess I'm still guilty of overpromising from time to time. Take this book, for example. I've sometimes been late in delivering chapters, much to the annoyance of my editor. I'm not perfect when it comes to tackling new tasks. I preach one thing; sometimes I do another.

If you must delay a deadline or leave an order unfulfilled, announce it to your client as soon as you know it yourself. Anglos are far better at bringing up bad news than Latinos. We have a deep-seated reluctance to talk about anything we consider unpleasant. We hope for miracles, and miracles are at best uncommon. So if something goes wrong, confess quickly. Many times your client will help you work out a solution. Circumstances sometimes make it impossible to keep a promise. Reasonable people understand that. It has happened to everybody. So be cool.

Just remember: deliver what you say you will, tackle problems immediately if they might force you to break your promises, and clients will return. Don't deliver, and clients will find someone who does.

10. Successful Latinos Balance Their Lives Between Work and Family

Just last week I went with my wife, Kathy, to see a high school football game where my stepson John was playing. When the game was over, I noticed a small boy—he could not have been more than four—sitting alone in the stands. While the game was going on he was okay, but now that the spectators were leaving, he began to cry, patently scared. Several people close by tried to comfort him, but he was too terrified for comfort, and his wails grew louder and louder.

Just then his father appeared at the foot of the stands and began running up toward him. The boy saw, gave a shriek, and allowed himself to be carried down to Daddy, who put his arms around him and simply hugged him until the boy stopped crying.

I was close enough to hear. "I'm sorry," the man was saying. "*Todo está bien*—everything's fine. I got stuck in the bathroom. I didn't know the game was over, or I'd have hurried back even faster. You know I'd never really leave you. Never leave you alone for long. You were a good boy to wait for me."

In those few minutes I saw a caring father. He might have put on his macho hat and said, "Don't cry. Act like a big boy." He might have been embarrassed at his own transgression and taken it out on his son. Instead he let the boy express his fear, waited patiently until it passed. He simply was there for his child, giving comfort.

A small incident, but it touched me deeply. That man was first and foremost a family man, a father. Not the kind of father I was to my children when I was in my twenties and first starting in business. Then I was too ambitious, too preoccupied, too focused on becoming successful to realize that *real* success lies in family as much as work. Whatever riches I made did not compensate for the fact that for years I was alienated from my first four children (I haven't made the same mistake with my two later ones). We're close once more, but it has taken many years of family counseling to begin to heal the pain I caused them.

Compassion, love, understanding, the value of family: they are all built into the Latino soul. Alas, when we get into Anglo-style business, we tend to play down these values—we "overcompensate" for them, getting wrapped up in our work and sacrificing family for career success.

It's the most costly mistake you can make, and if you learn nothing else from this chapter, learn that. My friend Doctor Fernando Avila has mastered the art of combining work and family perfectly. He is an anesthesiologist, hugely in demand, yet he and his wife Beverly carefully carve out time for their three children (two in high school, one in junior high) by a) taking them to school every morning; b) planning family vacations, family parties, and big gatherings where all the kids' friends are invited; c) making sure time is allocated at night to help with homework and on the weekends to do anything they wish together with their friends. *Es una familia unida*—indeed, a close-knit family.

I urge that no matter what your business, you write down "family appointments" on your calendar and stick to them just as though they were business appointments. Stephan Rechtschaffen, who wrote a book on the importance of changing the gears of time in one's life, recommends setting aside a day or a weekend when the family can dictate anything they want and you must obey, no matter what else you had in mind. He also has a game called Swept Away in which one spouse takes the other along without telling where they're going.

No matter what approach you use, make sure family and work are in balance. Don't think that you can stick to business now and bond with your children when you retire. You may end up having children who, like you, are aloof and detached, valuing "other commitments" over closeness and emotional gratification.

Believe me. I tried the business-only route and it took years to repair the rift with my children.

11. Successful Latinos Know When to Let Go

Entrepreneurs are driven by business, obsessed with it; that may be why you're reading this book. Many of us Latinos start small, having no business to inherit or business tradition to follow. At first, we do everything ourselves: manufacturing, selling, negotiating, keeping the books, borrowing, even *sweeping*. But then, when the business starts to grow, we hire others to help us.

If we're *patrones*, we continue to want to do it all—*hacerlo todo*. We're dissatisfied with those we hire. "They simply can't get it right," we think. We give them orders, expecting them to do everything exactly the way we do it. When they add their own creativity to the job, we criticize them, chastise them. And we may let them go, but often what's really happening is that *we* can't let go.

Yet letting go is an essential act if you're going to be truly successful. The willing delegation of responsibility, the recognition of the fact that you can't do it all and that *others will do it differently from you*, is fundamental to your business career.

It's natural to want to hold on. After all, the business is your baby, your vision, your goal, *es todo tuyo*! By assigning responsibility to others, you're admitting someone else (even a number of people) into your dream. You become more encourager than doer—the captain of the team, not the sole player.

Remember: no matter how specific you are in your assignments to your people, the job will *never* come back exactly the way you envisioned it. Individual people have individual methods, individual *eyes*, and if they're any good at all, they'll perforce add a piece of themselves to the mix.

Learning this was a painful process for me. When I started my advertising agency, I was writer, artist, producer, accountant, and salesman. When the agency flourished, I had to turn to others (even though I was neglecting my family in order to do as much as possible myself) and indeed let go of what I loved the most, the creative part, because bringing in new business had to come first.

I'd demonstrate, oversee. Almost invariably I *hated* what the creative team produced, and time and again I'd make them redo their work. "Incompetents!" I'd think to myself.

Once, though, we didn't have time to make changes. A client wanted us to present a new campaign in a hurry, so even though I was unhappy with what my team produced, probably because it was not *my* idea, I had no alternative but to accept it.

"You come to the client meeting with me," I pouted. "It's your work. If you think it's so good, *you* present it."

Strangely, rather than being cowed, they were delighted. Throughout the meeting I kept quiet while they presented what I considered to be "so-so" work, and when they finished I turned to the client, expecting a thumbs-down.

"Wonderful!" the client cried. "That's the best creative proposal I've ever seen. Where did you get these guys, Lionel? They're terrific!"

At that moment, I grew up. It was the most powerful business lesson I could have learned. I knew that in the future my job would be totally different—to focus on long-term planning and new business, and to leave the rest to the very capable people I'd hired. There were, I realized, people who were just as good as me, albeit in a different way, and a team is much more effective—*todos juntos somos más*—than any one individual.

When you're a mature manager, you'll realize that your main job is to inspire and motivate. You will become chief strategist, not chief craftsman.

My hero, the advertising guru David Ogilvy, once said, "Hire people brighter and more talented than you. If necessary, pay them more than you pay yourself." I've consistently tried to employ people more talented than I. Maybe someday I'll pay them more. But not yet.

12. Successful Latinos Persevere After Failure

My stepson John's team lost the football game (the one where I saw the crying child) by a score of 42–6. After the game he joined us in the car. I expected him to be devastated by the embarrassing trouncing. Instead he was delighted. His own performance had improved significantly over the way he'd played the week before.

John's dream is to play quarterback for Alabama. This was his second game as starting quarterback for his high school freshman team. And 42–6 was indeed a bit better than the previous week, when his team had lost 40–0 and he had been intercepted twice and sacked four times, with his team making no first downs during the entire game. This week he had passed for a touchdown, had a run of twenty yards, was responsible for five first downs, and kept the game close for a half. After the game he studied the videotape my wife had taken. All he saw was the good stuff. No question about it, he had improved, and that made him very, very happy.

The qualities of all successful entrepreneurs are exemplified in this story. John is an optimist. He saw the good plays he had made and focused on them. He visualized himself as quarterback and knew that with every game he would only get better. He was willing to accept suggestions from his family, and he is learning from his mistakes. Next week, or the week after, or the week after that, he will lead his team to victory. He will be a quarterback simply and precisely because he refuses to let failure stop him.

In fact, everybody fails during the course of a career. But the successful entrepreneur will use failure as a lesson, analyzing it with total honesty, and he will be better prepared for the next encounter.

One of my biggest disappointments in business came nine years ago. On December 15 we were approached by Gillette, then the most prestigious account we could have dreamed of having. They asked us to present our ideas on January third. December 15! January 3! It meant that fifteen of us had to work nonstop through the holiday season, giving up our Christmas and watching New Year's fireworks from the office window.

The presentation we put together was superb—the best we had ever done. And we were sure, going into the meeting, that we would win the account. But we lost it to a bigger and better-known firm.

"*¿Como puede ser?*"—how could it be? We were stunned. They *couldn't* have done as well, we felt. Where had we gone wrong?

After days of study, we figured it out. Our presentation was fine; we had lost to the better-known firm precisely *because* they were better known. A company like Gillette couldn't associate with an ad agency that was not the most prestigious available. *"Querían lo mejor y la más grande"*—they wanted the biggest and the best.

We learned that we had to concentrate on creating a positive spin for our agency, in effect promoting *ourselves* before we could promote others. We made sure our name appeared in trade publications; we let reporters into our offices, made friends with them, shared our methods and decisions. Soon they were not only writing about us but, we felt, rooting for us between the lines. My dream was to create the largest Hispanic advertising agency in America. We had not reached that yet (we were about fourth or fifth), but we were becoming the *best known* and we were on our way. We had rebounded from failure.

⤸

You can see how these twelve traits intertwine, how each must become an integral part of the whole, the successful businessperson. I've painted the traits in broad strokes. You'll have to incorporate them into your own life based on your goals and desires, your ambition, and your passion.

They are the principles I swear by and live by. Make them part of you. And succeed!

CHAPTER 5

THE ANGLO BUSINESSPERSON

¿Amigo o enemigo?

Many of us Latinos tend to stereotype Anglo businesspersons. We look upon them as exclusionary, tribal beings interested in doing business only with their "own kind." We believe this with such conviction that often we don't even *try* to break into their business or social world. And if we do, it is with a sense of trepidation and distrust that renders us less able to enjoy the success that could come our way.

Let's face it. We too have our prejudices, our "attitude." We too feel more comfortable doing business with people who look like us, talk like us, act like us. Many of us are convinced that "our way" is best and only "our people" can live up to our expectations.

The feeling is quite natural. Most people feel most comfortable with those who are most familiar. For example, not long ago Pat Legan, former chairman of the San Antonio Greater Chamber of Commerce (an organization that is about 10 percent Hispanic in a city that is almost 60 percent Hispanic), approached me when I was head of the San Antonio Hispanic Chamber of Commerce (5 percent Anglo). He had an idea: that we might merge into one body of businesspeople (50 percent Hispanic, 50 percent Anglo) for the greater good of our city. But despite Legan's and my advocacy of working as one, the board of my Hispanic Chamber of Commerce overwhelmingly rejected the idea. "We'd be chewed up," they felt. "*Nos comen vivos*. In no time, we'll be taken over by the Anglos." And even though there would be equal representation on the board and among the membership, there was a deep sense of mistrust. Unspoken was the feeling that, "this is our Chamber and we don't want anyone else butting into our business."

In truth, the average Latino businessperson is just about as racist as the average Anglo businessperson. Nothing unusual or extraordinary about that. Anglos feel more comfortable with other Anglos; we feel more comfortable among other Latinos. But the successful business leaders of the future know that very soon America will be only half white or Anglo-Saxon; the other half will be black, yellow, brown, and red. They must embrace diversity because exclusivity endangers the long-term prospects of their business.

"It's not that we're bigoted," Pat Legan told me when he approached me about merging the two Chambers, "it's that we commit a far greater sin—we don't even *think* about you." Pat was insightful and understanding of this dilemma, but when he and his peers *did* think about us, we turned our backs. Not very smart. Only by changing our mind-set can we make them change theirs.

⤳

Few people of any race think of *themselves* as racists or bigots. "*¿Yo? Nunca podría ser racista*"—Moi, a racist? If they are prejudiced, they don't see it. They see themselves as fair people who just "know" that their way of life (or religion, or culture) is the right one. As for the others, well, it's best to leave them alone, to let them behave in their different (i.e., inferior) ways. To many people, it makes no sense to try to get to know different nationalities or to understand different cultures. The task hardly seems worth the effort. If others' skin color, accent, dress is different, then *they're* different. Just let them be.

But no matter how much we may try to point up our external differences, every human being is pretty much the same inside. The fundamental human impetuses of love, family, a secure life, generosity of spirit are common to us all. We all have similar hopes, dreams, and fears.

We all want to be accepted, and it's easier to be accepted in our own group than in another's. We all want to succeed, and it's easiest to succeed if we're with our own kind. And so we become insular and adopt a kind of racism that is both unconscious and unacknowledged. Unknowingly we accept the stereotypes and perhaps think there's a grain of truth in the lies that overt racists spread about groups other than their own.

A few years ago I was doing research for Budweiser beer on Latino male beer-drinking habits, a job that took me to many different bars in different cities where there is a large Latino population. In New York, I found myself in Spanish Harlem with lots of beer-loving Latino males.

I'd been warned about Harlem and how scary it was, but to my surprise I felt particularly comfortable there. While most of the men had darker skin than mine ("black" Dominicans and Puerto Ricans), we were obviously from the same roots and we certainly spoke the same language. Besides, the men I interviewed seemed to enjoy the contact. They were glad to accept a free beer from me, and to explain why they preferred one brand of beer to another, why they drank at all, and what kind of companionship resulted from a couple of hours spent at a bar.

I visited about five bars that afternoon, taking lengthy notes, and emerged from the last one at around seven o'clock. It was a cold March night, and very dark. I couldn't find a taxi, so I headed for the nearest subway.

Suddenly I became aware of a strange phenomenon: The streets looked the same and the people looked the same; the same workers were coming home for dinner and the same kids playing in the streets—but now everybody was speaking English. I had walked right into Black Harlem! The passersby were African-Americans. Gone was my sense of comfort and pleasure, my feeling of belonging.

"*¡Dios mío!*" I ducked gratefully into the subway. Now Harlem *was* scary!

Why? Because from deep in my subconscious the feeling of "otherness," of racism, had surfaced.

A close friend of mine, a highly religious man, had a similar experience. He was in Los Angeles, driving along the freeway, when a car driven by a black youth, with another beside him and a third in the back, pulled alongside. The driver motioned my friend to roll down his window. My friend smiled at them, but sped away, feeling very uncomfortable. The car followed. He turned off at an exit ramp. Still the car followed. He came to a red light, stopped. The car stopped at his side. One of the youths got out of the car and approached. My friend locked the door and kept his window rolled up. He waited to see a gun pointed at his head. Instead he saw a smile.

"You dropped your hubcap when you got on the freeway," the young man said when my friend hesitantly rolled down his window. He handed it to my friend. "We picked it up for you, but you're a tough man to catch up with."

The two of us discussed our mutual reactions. Both of us were surprised at our behavior, even a little ashamed—*nos dio vergüenza*. We realized that prejudice exists to some degree in all of us, no matter who we are, and that only by being aware of it in ourselves can we work to eradicate it.

⌇

Nowhere is stereotyping and its attendant prejudice more visible than in the business world. When I was on a task force for the Hispanic Chamber, we worked hard to get large corporations to hire small Latino firms for much of their outsourcing. I personally went to the CEOs of a number of Anglo firms to ask for their cooperation.

"But we *have* been cooperating" was the universal response. Indeed, the firms—many of which had created special departments specifically to attract minority suppliers—had sent out requests for bids to more than a hundred minority-owned businesses. None had responded!

Algo no está bien, we decided—something's not right. We interviewed the heads of the Latino companies and asked why they had not bid.

"It would have been useless," one business owner explained, speaking for all of them. "I got the request all right, but I didn't respond. The job would have gone to an Anglo no matter what my bid. They were just playing politics."

I was dumbfounded. The chasm between Anglos and Latinos was wider than I imagined.

In my consumer research around the country, I had witnessed racism even among Latinos when discussing each other ("Cubans are arrogant"; "Mexicans are poor"; "Puerto Ricans are apathetic"; "Central Americans aren't as sophisticated as South Americans"). I'd seen stereotypical attitudes regarding religious groups, age groups, economic groups, gays and heterosexuals. In one political focus group, a fist fight broke out over the way a black man was "looking at" a white man.

But this case seemed to me particularly self-defeating. The Latino firms had joined the Chamber of Commerce for the very purpose of increasing their business. Now that a new business opportunity was presented to them, they spurned it. They had no real evidence the Anglo firms were playing politics; they simply imagined it, accepted the stereotypical view, and turned away. Amazing!

We inaugurated a series of workshops for Anglos and Latinos in which they could air their differences and desires. We followed with social mixers, dances, dinners for businesspeople and their spouses, all in an effort to get a dialogue going, to develop friendship and trust—*para conocernos mejor.*

More business resulted, but not nearly enough. Today a new generation of Chamber leadership is working just as hard as I did to bring down the barriers, but some Latinos may still feel that Anglos are blocking their way, and sometimes they are right. Yet in business, it's profits that count, and the profit motive, believe it or not, is usually stronger than prejudice. If everyone works together, it can work for everybody's profit.

As Latinos we *must* believe we can succeed together. It's true, and it's self-defeating to deny it. There are really no tyrants or monsters out there. There are just imperfect businesspeople—Anglo, black, Asian, whatever. They love, fear, dream, have ambitions, fail or succeed just like us. They are capable of trust and friendship—indeed, they want it. They are people.

So how do we bridge the gap among imperfect people?

Well, one way *not* to bridge it is to sit back and "let them come to us."

Don't wait for a corporation to contact you. Reach out. Be the first to make the contact. Prepare a list of projects, examples of your previous work, your competitive prices. Show your willingness to do more *con gusto* to prove that your firm is the one for the job.

Anticipate friendship and trust. Remember: you get what you expect. If you expect rejection, you'll get rejected. Go in expecting you'll get the business, and there's a good chance you will. I'm talking about attitude here, self-confidence and mutual respect. If you can show how you can contribute to your prospect's profits, I guarantee you success. In American business it's profits, not racism, that drive the corporate decisions.

～

This attitude stuff is all well and good, you might say. *But . . .*

I'm not blind—*no estoy ciego.* There *is* bigotry, racism, and prejudice out there. Still, things are not always that cut-and-dried.

Let me give you an example. There are three small firms—all Anglo—vying for a large outsource contract offered by a Fortune 500 corporation. All three receive a request for a proposal. The playing field seems level on the surface, but the owner of one of the small businesses worked for that same corporation until three years ago and left with many friends and an excellent reputation. This fellow, in addition to preparing a fine proposal, makes personal calls to his friends inside, stressing how much he wants the business. He gets helpful information the others don't have simply because they didn't ask. On the day of the oral presentations, he has a friendly audience.

All three Anglo companies are equally capable—but who's going to get the business? You guessed it! The one with more friends. Is this prejudice? Is it favoritism? Is it good fortune? Probably a combination of all three. It happens every day. It happens in your family. It's human nature.

It's the same when you own a "minority" company going into competition with Anglo firms. The Anglos have the advantage because they are more like "them." They will be more likely to have the friends, the inside information. So you must be better, cheaper, or faster to have a fighting chance.

The point is that many times what we interpret as racism is not necessarily so; it's more complex than that. It could be that the other guy has the friends, the other guy knows what pressure to exert, or the other guy "speaks the same language." Don't just blame it on "prejudice." If you don't win out, learn why you lost and keep trying. All good work eventually pays off. Just be better or cheaper or faster—you don't have to be all three.

It worked for me when I started out in business. Here I was, a Mexican kid twenty-three years old, wanting to do artwork for the Anglo advertising agencies in San Antonio. I had no college education. I had no experience in advertising. I was a sign painter!

But I did have talent, a desire to succeed, motivation inspired by the Napoleon Hill course—and the need to feed a wife and four kids. So I decided to be all three: the best, the fastest, *and* the cheapest graphic artist in San Antonio. *El mejor, el más rápido, y el más barato.* How could I go wrong?

Here's what I did:

- I prepared a portfolio of my work to demonstrate its quality (*the best*).
- I took a two-week vacation from my regular job at Texas Neon to make calls on ad agencies and printers. (Yes, they were all Anglos.)
- I made four appointments a day (two in the morning, two in the afternoon), which I arranged over the phone. If a company did not invite me to come, I showed up anyway and waited—sometimes for hours—until someone would see me.

- I guaranteed next-morning (8 A.M.) delivery of all artwork (*the fastest*).
- I guaranteed the best price. In fact, I told them that when I delivered the work it would be accompanied by a blank invoice. They could fill in *any* price they felt the work was worth (*the cheapest*).

And I made a deal with myself: I would not leave their office until I had a job, no matter how small, where I could *prove* that I would make good on my guarantees.

Most of the time, the reaction went something like this:

"That's a compelling proposition, but I don't have anything for you right now," or ". . . but we already have a graphic artist and designer. We don't need another."

I persisted: "Surely you must have *something*. What about your own new business prospects? Give me their names, and I'll design a new logo for them so you can have something to show as a door-opener. Only if you get the business do you need to pay me." I was so insistent that about half the time I'd walk out with a job. When I didn't get work, I'd go back again and again, showing off the work I was doing for others and telling them of my success with my new clients.

Soon I had so much business I had to quit Texas Neon. *Plus* I didn't have to make a new-business call for nine years after that. *(Imaginate: ¡nueve años!)* Of course I had to work like hell. I'd pick up the jobs during the day and together with my first partner, Lupe Garcia, work till 1 or 2 in the morning to live up to my next-day promise. We loved it! My income quadrupled, my business was off the ground.

Nobody cared that I was Mexican, that I didn't have a college education, that my father ran a laundry, that I lived on the west side of town. All they cared about was that I could help them earn a greater profit. And guess what: there was no evidence of prejudice, bigotry, or discrimination. I had won my jobs by being best, fastest, cheapest. At our agency today, we're still the best and often the fastest. But we're no longer cheapest. We've earned the right to charge what the best deserves.

There's no question that Latinos have to fight harder, prepare more carefully, charge less, and deliver more quickly when starting out in the American business world.

We can resent it, in which case we can retreat to the safety of a low-level job, grumbling all the while about "unfairness." Or we can accept it as a challenge, in which case persistence, patience, and preparation will eventually pay off.

The Anglo businessperson is neither friend nor foe. In most cases, he or she *wants* to be our partner—if we can prove what *we* know is true: that we're as good as anybody and better than most.

But we can only be good if we learn to avoid the traps that lie in our path.

CHAPTER 6

THE TRAPS

Ten mucho cuidado

Roberto Goizueta. He is the most successful of all Latino businessmen—in fact, one of the most successful businesspeople, period. He is the keeper of the world's best-known brand. And he's been recognized by *Fortune* magazine as the CEO who produced the most shareholder wealth during his tenure. His story stands as a model for all of us. I tell it now because I know of no one who better avoided the traps many of us fall into (I count seven of them), and if we cannot precisely copy his career, at least we can learn from it.

Roberto was born in Cuba to middle-class parents, held a job as a chemist at the Coca-Cola plant in Havana, and with his wife fled to the United States when Castro came to power. They arrived with forty dollars in their pockets—and a commodity Roberto claims was far more valuable than money (*"más valioso que dinero"*): one hundred shares of Coca-Cola stock.

The stock "was ten times more important than anything else in my life," Roberto says. "It was a shocker. I realized it was the only thing I had, and it brought me a sense of humility, a sense of the impermanence of material things."

The stock was for him a talisman. It was something tangible—the only material thing he had to hold on to—and it made him feel that he was part owner of a great corporation, even if it was only an infinitesimal part.

He called it "shareholder equity," and from the moment he arrived he was filled with the sense that his mission was to make that equity grow, not only for himself but for *all* shareholders. He felt that to help raise the value of Coca-Cola stock, he had to *work* at Coca-Cola, so he got a low-ranking job in the technical branch. From there he was promoted to jobs in the legal department, external affairs, and administration. In all of them, he made integrity his watchword. "I never set a goal to be this or that," he said later, though his overreaching goal remained constant. "I always believed that if you do the best you can, *alguien lo notará*—someone will notice it sooner or later. You just have to hope it's sooner."

In his case, someone did notice. Robert Woodruff, CEO of Coca-Cola from the 1950s through the early 1980s, liked Roberto's style, his work ethic, his curiosity about all aspects of the business. He began to take the young man to lunch to teach him about the business and to discuss ideas with him. Soon the two men would spend hours together after work, and Woodruff found he could rely on his protégé to tell him the truth frankly and honestly, even when he disagreed with his boss. Particularly, Woodruff liked the young man's toughness and sense of tradition and decorum.

So close did their relationship become, so thoroughly grounded was Goizueta in the company, that Woodruff groomed him as his successor, and in 1981, when Woodruff retired, Goizueta became CEO of Coca-Cola Worldwide.

Now he was able to truly attain his goal. From 1981 to 1996, he created fifty-nine *billion* dollars in additional dividends for Coca-Cola stockholders. That's more than any CEO in American history. How's *that* for a Latino businessman in the United States?

↪

In 1994, Goizueta was the keynote speaker at the National Convention of Latino Businessmen and Businesswomen, speaking to us eloquently in Spanish. "I come to you not as CEO of a global organization," he said, "but as a Latino businessperson just like you—*vengo aquí como uno de ustedes.*"

In truth, he wasn't *just* like us—he was quite a bit grander. But he stood as a reminder to all of us that any degree of success is possible for a Latino in the business world. He did not flaunt his heritage, though I know he is proud of it. He was there as a kind of Everybusinessman, a man who by recognizing early on what is important, and by keeping focused on his goal, was able to avoid the traps that lie in the road to Hispanic business success.

"A lot of executives can intellectualize the process," says George M. C. Fisher, CEO of Eastman Kodak. "Roberto can follow through."

Roberto Goizueta avoided several traps in his rise at Coca-Cola. There are other traps he did not come up against—but you might.

⤸

The "They Don't Like Latinos" Chip on the Shoulder

When young Roberto and his bride arrived in America, they spoke no English and had no contacts. They could have been bitter, could have said, "They don't like Latinos here, so we can expect little help," could have become angry, disappointed, disoriented. Instead they pressed forward, concentrating on a goal, and for purposes of beginning a business life "forgot about" their heritage, much as it meant to them.

Roberto knew that to increase the equity of his shares in Coca-Cola—the number one brand of soft drink in the world—he couldn't be involved in a mom-and-pop business; he had to go to the source and work from within. He had a focused goal and relied on his belief that he was just as good as anyone else—that if he worked hard, studied hard, and committed himself to his vision, things would take care of themselves and he would be rewarded with success. Others would notice what he was doing, notice *him,* not because he was Latino but because his achievements were as good or better than those of his colleagues.

He had his ups and downs at Coke, to be sure. Coca-Cola suffered a colossal business failure when they introduced new "improved" Coke to a country that much preferred the "real thing." He and his management team owned up to their misjudgment. They retrenched and refocused and made sure that an invigorated marketing approach more than made up for its losses. Not once did he make excuses. He never even considered "the press is giving Coke bad publicity because I'm Latino" (as crazy as it seems, some Latinos actually blame such setbacks on their ethnicity); there was only an admission of a learning experience and a turn to a better future.

I think Roberto was at his very best in this period. Too often I've seen Latinos blaming others when things get really tough. If you think the world's against you, then the world *will* be against you. In failure you have only yourself to blame—just as in success you can take a large share of the credit.

The Minority/Disadvantaged Land Mine

Being a member of a minority certainly did not hold Roberto Goizueta back—nor did it help him. And ideally, of course, race should not matter in either the search for a job or one's success once it is found.

But many Latinos use their Latino-ness as their road to riches. They rely on government set-asides (which are harder and harder to get these days) and, once having obtained them, they become noncompetitive. They relax, oblivious to the fact that this was meant as a jump start. They forget that, like all contracts, government contracts have time limits—that once the government contract runs out, the teat is gone.

I have a friend who obtained one of the best of all the government contracts under the 8A set-aside program. He was to provide consulting services for several military bases across the country. The contract was an enormous one. It allowed him and his family a grand lifestyle and his future was secure—*todo estaba seguro.*

For ten years.

There was a stop date in the government contract; it expired after a decade, the government assuming that by that time my friend would have built up a business he could run on his own. But my friend either forgot about the stop date or went into a state of denial as it approached. He did not do the *real* work needed to look for new avenues for his business, figuring that somehow the government contract would be renewed. He did nothing innovative that would attract private investors once the government contract ran out.

So precisely ten years after the start-up date, my friend found himself without any business at all. The government awarded the contract to someone else, and my friend had nothing to turn to, no alternative plan. He was horrified. He was still convinced he was "disadvantaged" and therefore deserved more than what he had already gotten.

There is, of course, nothing wrong with availing yourself of set-aside programs; they can be immensely helpful. But you must remember that they are at best start-ups, that they run out. Eventually, like all businesspeople in America, the Latino businessperson will be on his or her own. A set-aside program can actually slow you down! It's quite possible to be far more successful "on your own" from the beginning. If you can walk without a crutch, why use it? It only weakens you. *La muleta a veces debilita.*

The "You Can't Fight City Hall" Syndrome

"City halls," corporate and political, do exist. Bureaucracies are just as firmly entrenched in business as they are in government, and just as resistant to change. Like federal, state, and city agencies, businesses have their "set ways"; even CEOs, like presidents and governors and mayors, often find themselves unable to scrap old ideas or old methods of operation. Security prevails over innovation, the past over the future, what has worked over what might work better.

We Latinos are particularly reluctant to engage in the wearisome battle for change—we don't like to challenge the system. Our slave heritage (probably abetted by our parents) has taught us that "making waves," with the high visibility that entails, is a risky business. We would be much better off letting things stand, we're told, cooperating with the bureaucracy rather than confronting it. "Corporations don't change," we allow ourselves to think, "so why go through an exercise in futility?" The changes probably wouldn't be accepted anyway, and why get in trouble with the system?

Yet we must change our attitude for two principal reasons. First, because we *can* make a difference if there needs to be a difference— *"Juntos somos la diferencia,"* as the Anheuser Busch ads put it. And second, because if we don't express ourselves we will never be heard; part of us will be silenced, and we will become "invisible."

I know it's tough. I know it can indeed lead to frustration. And yes, in bureaucracies it's more difficult for a Latino than an Anglo to find a sympathetic ear. But sometimes it's easier for a Latino to be heard. Many minorities have made huge differences within their corporations just because of their minority status.

I never said business success is easy. But I do say it's *possible,* within our grasp. And unless we are prepared to fight for it—by speaking up at meetings, by presenting new ideas to management and clients and prospective clients, by recommending change when we see its possibilities—then we will remain "invisible," with all that implies.

When he became CEO in 1981, Roberto Goizueta knew that the soft-drink industry was lagging (*Newsweek* called it "graying"). No more than a three-percent annual growth was projected—and the bureaucracy at Coca-Cola, established over years of success, was satisfied that this was enough.

But Roberto was *dis*satisfied. So he formed focus groups of soft-drink customers to ask for new ideas, presented a new mission statement, brought to everyone in the company a sense that they were *owners.* He communicated the very feeling that had inspired him from the beginning. He instituted a series of changes in marketing, distribution, and manufacturing that overall raised the value of Coca-Cola stock year after year. Roberto took risks—and thereby brought to a great but rapidly fossilizing company a new spirit and a new sense of purpose.

The "I'll Be Happy with Just a Small Piece of the Pie" Attitude

Our heritage tells us we must be grateful for small favors. "Going for it all" is not in the Latino mind-set. *"El que mucho abarca, poco aprieta"* (he who goes for too much winds up with little) is a familiar attitude, instilled in our ancestors by the *conquistadores.* Yet Roberto went for it all. So have thousands of other entrepreneurs. So can you.

I had been taught at the Napoleon Hill school that it's as easy to go for a million dollars as to go for a thousand—all you have to do is believe. Nothing could be more true. Early in the life of our agency, the "million dollars" we decided to try for was the Coca-Cola account. When we pitched them, they gave us an opportunity, albeit a small one: a modest fee for manning the booths at various conventions, extolling the virtues of allied products, and handing out advertising literature.

That was our "foot in the door" to Coke's Atlanta headquarters, where we got to know their advertising and marketing people—and made friends with them.

Coke had been using a New York–based advertising agency for five years. We thought their ads were awful (no bias there!). We who were much smaller and much less famous decided to go into competition with the Madison Avenue shop. We did months of research and kept coming up with ideas for advertisements and promotions, which we presented to our clients at their Atlanta headquarters every time we updated them on our booth assignments.

Coke agreed that our ads were good, and after a year we were invited to make a presentation. The result was that they decided to split the business. We would get the Diet Coke and Sprite accounts (one-quarter of the overall business); the New York agency would retain Coca-Cola Classic.

"No—eso no," I said. To the surprise of the Coca-Cola executives (and, initially, of my partners), I turned them down flat. I told them we were good enough to be awarded the entire account.

"Lionel, be patient," they said. "Do well with the smaller brands and soon you can have it all."

I could understand their position. We were still a small agency and still unproven. But I could sense they were unhappy with their "no-risk" New York agency. Besides, we were more competent. My partners could smell victory, so they chimed in: "If you agree we're the better agency, you owe it to yourselves to assign us the whole business."

We argued, pleaded, and discussed alternatives for half an hour, but I stood fast. Then they went to another room for a private conference. Fifteen minutes later they returned. "Okay," they announced, and gave us the entire account. They would go with the more worthy agency. Our determination and belief in ourselves had paid off.

That account was worth five million dollars then. It was worth thirty million eight years later. I felt then that we had gone past our apprenticeship, that we no longer needed to be the cheapest. We didn't even have to be the fastest every time—only the very best. And from that experience, I learned some valuable lessons:

- Believe in what you do—*Ten fe en ti mismo.*
- Go for it all (wear a "no-fear" T-shirt if you have to).
- Once you're established and believe you're the best, ask high fees, sometimes the highest; the best deserve them.
- Those who haggle over price but agree to "pay you when you've proved yourself" tend to forget that promise. When they're tight-fisted at the beginning, they're tight-fisted forever more.
- Don't bargain for less than you're worth. Your pride is more important than an immediate sale.
- Take the risk that your prospective client will opt for someone else. If that's the way they feel, let them! Save yourself the frustration and the anger. You'll close fewer deals, but

you'll have kept your standards high, and your clients will be happier because they chose you.

Remember: I'm talking about your position *after* you're established. Before that, you'll have to compromise, hustle, prove yourself worthy.

The "Time Takes Care of Everything" Excuse

Twenty years ago the Latino community had a rallying cry: *The 1980s will be the decade of the Hispanic—la década del hispano.*

Working out a campaign for Coors beer as the 1980s approached, our firm adopted the slogan and persuaded the brewer to begin an aggressive campaign linking Coors to the "decade of the Hispanic." The ads ran on Spanish-language radio and television, and the sale of Coors rose among Hispanics. We were proud of our achievement.

Not so fast, Lionel! I had also advised Coors to feature the phrase on a series of billboards, and these backfired. Since the 1980s was to be the decade of the Hispanic, by implication it would *not* be the decade of the Anglo—and Anglos saw the slogan on the highways and quite correctly resented it. Some Coors retailers even refused to sell the beer and brought it back to the distributors. Coors stuck by its campaign and eventually won back its lost Anglo business, but I had learned a lesson. In my impetuousness I had moved too fast, too arrogantly. In the words of Pat Legan, I had committed the great sin of "not even thinking about them." I should have kept the campaign on Spanish media only and not put it on billboards "in the Anglo's face."

I was reminded of another ad campaign, also for Coors beer, early in my career. This one was a series of double-page magazine pictures, one of which showed a New Mexico ranch where a young Hispanic man looked over his domain. The copy told readers that the ranch had previously been worked by his father for its Anglo owner but now belonged to the son. *"El tiempo arregla todo,"* the tag line read—time takes care of everything. The ad was beautiful and won many creative awards, but it was also based on a stereotype.

Time doesn't. Sometimes we must plunge ahead, as I did on the later Coors campaign, even if it's risky. We and only we are masters of our time; we must use it. If we wait for time, it will take care of nothing. Time does not right injustice or make unfairness fair. Contrary to what the Latino *dicho* says, *el tiempo* NO *arregla todo.*

In business, we have to make things happen. We need to create our own timetable, our own agenda. That is why I advocate defined goals and five-year plans to achieve them.

Author Karen Salmansohn (with apologies to Oscar Hammerstein II) advises her readers to complete this verse:

> Fish gotta swim,
> Birds gotta fly,
> Serial killers gotta kill,
> *I've* gotta _____

What *is* it that you have to do? Increase shareholder profits like Roberto Goizueta? Create the *right* ad, not just any ad, like we did at our agency? Save a dying college like Lou Agnese? Write? Teach? Coach? Bake? Succeed in the business you're best at? You must decide what it is that you have to do. And once you've decided, don't wait; as the great Nike slogan says, "just do it." Time won't bring it to you. You must get it for yourself.

The "Don't Make Waves" White Flag

This is a close cousin to the can't-fight-city-hall mind-set. We Latinos tend to *like* comfortable bureaucratic jobs. We don't automatically think that the highest paying jobs are part of our lives' equation. We'll sacrifice riches for safety. The risk is too great, the process too arduous, the routine too seductive to try to break out.

In the hundreds of focus groups I've conducted in the course of my work, I've seen the "don't make waves" flag raised again and again. Latinos are hesitant to express an opinion, even when we only ask them to give us their opinion about a product or service—even, in fact, when I've assured them that there are no right or wrong answers. In Anglo focus groups, it's hard to shut the people up; they can't wait to give their opinions. When Latinos are brought together, everyone is much more measured, reticent. They will wait for some brave soul to venture an opinion, and when that happens, the others usually agree. We've learned to conduct part of these focus groups through writing. Members are asked to fill out a form anonymously rating the product or advertisement on a scale from one to five *before* they begin to discuss its message. Also, when we show a commercial and ask for a reaction, we (and the client) sit behind one-way mirrors, judging the group's *real* opinion through body language and facial expressions. When do they nod in agreement? Smile? Look confused? Frown?

But opinions, the expression of ideas, are the basis for business success. You must speak—*tienes que hablar.* You must make your passionate beliefs heard. The follower cannot innovate, the timid cannot lead. Standing out from the crowd might mean briefly standing alone, but you will soon attract others. It's a matter of training. Give voice to your thoughts and you will be joined by a chorus. Remain silent and you don't exist.

The *"La Familia Primero"* Quicksand

A few years ago, Isabel Valdez, an eminent researcher, did a study working with both Anglo and Hispanic women aged twenty-five to forty. She asked both ethnic groups the following question:

"If you won ten thousand dollars in a lottery, would you a) invest it, b) remodel your kitchen, or c) take a vacation?"

Eighty-five percent of the Anglo women chose the vacation. But among the Hispanic women, nine out of ten said they would remodel the kitchen!

This is symptomatic of the Latino reflex that family comes first. It's a basic, strong belief in our culture. But it can be dangerous when it impedes your path to success.

To a Latino, keeping the family together is paramount, even if it means not sending a child with good high school grades away to college, even if it precludes travel to foreign countries (a different but equally important kind of education), even if it means hiring someone from the family to fill a job when a better qualified "outsider" is readily available. Consider these business situations, and then ask yourself, "How would I handle this? After all, it's family."

- Your brother-in-law, the comptroller, is $6,000 short: *¿ahora qué?*—now what?
- Your nephew who is always late asks for a week off with pay: *¿qué haces?*—what do you do?
- Your son "knows" how to double the business if you only let him handle it: *¿cómo lo ves?*—how do you see it?
- Your daughter wants you to hire her boyfriend: *¡caramba!*

Strangely, it's easier to form the business team with colleagues than with family members. That way family sentiments, biases, conflicts, and politics don't intrude.

Then what do you do about family members? Love them, spend time with them, cherish them. And, spouses sometime excepted, keep business and family separate. It's less stressful, and with few exceptions, more successful.

Having goals, avoiding traps, understanding your heritage, recognizing your strengths and weaknesses: all these are essential elements in your climb to success, but they are not enough.

It's time now to turn to practical considerations, the specific skills you will need to compete in the American business world.

And you can't really start without a good education.

CHAPTER 7

IT'S THE LACK OF EDUCATION, STUPID!

Es cuestión de educación

I heard it first from my parents, then from my teachers, then from relatives and friends: *"Cuando tienes tu educación, tienes todo"*—when you have your education, you have everything.

The statement is in the Latino air. Everybody knows it, everybody repeats it. So you'd think that, like Asians (who are top achievers in education), we'd be making monumental strides. You'd think that our concern for a better education would translate into real progress for our children.

But it's not happening. Not yet. According to the American Council of Education, between 1993 and 1994 (the last years for which we have figures) there is no indication of improvement. In fact, the Latino high school graduation rate actually *declined* four percent—from 61 percent to 57 percent. By contrast, among both Anglos and African-Americans twenty-five to twenty-nine, 87 percent hold high school diplomas. Of those Latinos who graduated, the percentage of men and women going to college went from 35 percent to 33 percent, most of them attending two-year programs. Only 9 percent of all Latinos have bachelor's degrees (as opposed to 23 percent of non-Latinos), 6 percent earn associate degrees, 3 percent master's degrees, 2.3 percent doctorates. In San Antonio, my hometown, the high school dropout rate is the highest of all minority groups. This figure varies slightly from city to city but hovers at 50 percent nationwide.

In short, even as our families stress the importance of education, even as corporations and political leaders put education above any other national priority, and even as Latino focus groups unanimously announce that education is the number one concern, there has been little improvement in Latino participation in higher education in the last several years.

It's not that help isn't available. The National Hispanic Scholarship Fund, championed by the Anheuser-Busch company, has awarded 28,000 college scholarships. Groups such as the League of United Latin-American Citizens and individuals like Vikki Carr (through the Vikki Carr Scholarship Foundation) have given out millions of dollars in scholarship aid. Most major universities and, to a lesser extent, private colleges, have established outreach programs to attract Latino students, and many of them have scholarship money available for Latino applicants. Yet we don't seem to be making any progress.

Why? Given the importance we place on education, and our interest in seeing our children do well, you would think we'd have higher participation and achievement levels. *¿Qué pasa?*

Once more we must look to our roots.

When the Spanish *conquistadores* came to the Americas, education was the last thing they advocated for the Indians they ruled. They knew that an uneducated class would be an obedient class, that they would be far better off if the Indians remained subservient.

The church (the Spaniards' accomplices) agreed. They had the Indians tear down their places of worship and with the stones build huge cathedrals. "We'll take care of you," they said. "Listen to our God—the real God. This is what He wants for you." The church set up grade schools. Each parish had its own school. And from the time a Latino entered Catholic school, he and especially she were taught not to disobey and not to question. The governments and the religious institutions ran the schools virtually in tandem. Most Indian children were taught just enough to be able to learn the catechism, but the idea of further education was discouraged or actively squelched. A child of, say, ten was an economic asset to the family. Why continue with education when the child could be bringing in money by his or her sweat, in the shops or in the fields?

"Work is virtue. Poverty is virtue. God takes care of the virtuous. That is God's word," they said. "The family needs you to contribute. You must now leave school and help the family."

Thus when Latinos came to the United States, they carried no real tradition of higher education. Staying in school was not a priority; earning enough to help the family was. But Anglos, misunderstanding the Latino reluctance to continue in school, took it as a sign of laziness or lack of aspiration. "Latinos aren't smart," they thought. "Latinos aren't ambitious." And a stereotype was born.

⤺

In 1968 the University of Texas decided to open a branch in San Antonio. The man who would become its president summoned me and my partner Lupe Garcia to his office in its temporary headquarters and asked us to design a logo for the University of Texas at San Antonio.

"You know," he said, "this university will be of help to Latinos. You're so good with your hands. We'll be incorporating the teaching of Latino skills into our curriculum. Basket weaving. Pottery making. Why, our fine arts programs will enable your people to sell what they make along the River Walk."

We were appalled. But we were young kids, eager to please and eager for the assignment, so we shut up and designed the logo.

When the UTSA campus opened, the community (sans Latino involvement) heralded it as a solution for education in San Antonio. But it was located twenty miles from downtown San Antonio, far away from Latino neighborhoods. There was not even a bus route to get there. The message was clear: Since Latinos were not meant for higher education, why should anyone bother to provide it? Latinos should go to vocational schools (as I did; in those days, there was literally no alternative) to learn auto mechanics, body and fender work, printing—and, yes, basket weaving and pottery.

Only now, thirty years later, is the university opening a branch in urban San Antonio. But once again they've miscalculated. They anticipated 1,500 students. Nearly 4,000 have already enrolled. (Similarly, when a two-year college was built on San Antonio's south side, principally for Latinos, the enrollment was expected to be 4,000. It is 18,000!)

Clearly, the hunger for higher education exists. The young Latinos want it; their parents want it. But too often it is sidetracked by lack of tradition on our part and by stereotyping on the part of the Anglos. For example, I've made up the following situations, which can apply to junior-high, high school or college, and the typical Anglo and Latino reactions to them:

Situation	Anglo Reaction	Latino Reaction
Making the college decision	"You mean you're *not* going to college?"	"You mean you're going to *college*?"
Conflict with teacher; student complains	Parent assumes student is right, goes to school, shakes it up	Parent assumes kid is wrong, takes no action
Long line at registration	Student waits 20–30 minutes, leaves, phones registrar to protest	Student waits all day, comes back tomorrow
Parents' night	"What's happening with my kid?"	"Why am I here? What can I say to the teachers?"
Class participation	"My hand's up. Call on me."	"I didn't raise my hand. Please don't call on me."

When it comes to higher education, and especially graduate school, Latinos are truly living in a foreign world. It's for "them," not us, so we shun it, remain uninvolved. But we *do* care. We care a lot. And if we want to flourish in America, and if we want our piece of the Americano Dream, we must learn that higher education is meant for us too. Here, there's no church saying "don't."

A good education, of course, starts in the home. Parents can either build a desire for education in their children or stamp it out. Parents who, like the priests in the old country, preach that the children's obligation (and virtue) is to begin to work early, before they have finished school, are causing them profound injury. Parents who simply "hand over" their child to school authorities without investigating, without meeting with the teachers, and without questioning authority and fighting for what's best for the child are falling victim to the misguided teachings of our ancestors and forsaking their responsibility as parents. And fathers are just as important as mothers.

More Latino parents must do what Anglo and many African-American parents do. We must question the system when something doesn't seem right. We must push. We must fight. We must be there with them.

But even with the requisite parental push, *el empuje,* much of the responsibility for a child's academic success lies with the school and with the individual child.

Of the fifty percent of Latinos who do graduate from high school, most choose work over college, and the work is often that of barber, construction worker, clerical worker, technician—semiskilled jobs that pay little and offer few psychological rewards.

As noted, of the students who do choose college, most go to two-year community colleges. They equip themselves for higher-level white-collar jobs but deny themselves access to the top professions. Among those who graduate from a four-year school, many become grade school teachers, nurses, or social workers. There seems to be a deep desire among graduates to work in their own communities, to be part of *el movimiento.* In a way, they've developed a Hispanic peace-corps mentality, a sense that money and business success isn't as important as serving their own people.

I admire that attitude, and much progress has been made in our communities by those who have forged ahead. But the Latino community needs more: It needs scientists and engineers, mathematicians and economists, social scientists and historians and philosophers. (One important exception: there are many Hispanic doctors—in the helping professions there is no shortage of Latinos.)

"There's more out there," I want to shout, every time a child drops out of school, a high school graduate decides not to go to college, a student chooses a two-year college over a four-year one, a college graduate "settles" for a job as an underling. We must go further. On to graduate school to get our doctorates, so that we have more teachers at the university level. Otherwise, we'll be forever depending on role models not our own. We must have knowledge, and we must be able to impart it at *every* level.

Some organizations, fully aware of the problem, are doing something about it. The Hispanic Association of Colleges and Universities (HACU), the California Association of Chicanos in Higher Education (CACHE), and ASPIRA are all working with colleges and universities to help them understand the Latino community—and vice versa. In addition, magnet schools throughout the nation are bringing young Latinos into new environments where they will be exposed to nontraditional subjects and will be best able to use their talents. And I was delighted to learn that in Montgomery County, Maryland, there's a bilingual magnet school enrolling African-Americans and Anglos.

My brother Robert, who has been an educator all his life and is the source of inspiration for this chapter, agrees that Latino parents must play a crucial role in inspiring their children to go on to higher education. But he contends that the parents cannot do it alone. The education system itself must join them as partners.

A system, he says, owes its community a sincere, put-your-money-where-your-mouth-is commitment to the Latino student (as well as all other ethnic minorities) from elementary school to the graduate level. The institution must remake itself. It must exist for one purpose and one purpose only: to assure that *all* students will succeed. It must dedicate its money, its creativity, and the talents of its administrators and its teachers to that one endeavor. The institution must:

- *Understand* that ethnic-minority students have *special needs* and cater to those needs, both monetarily (by providing tuition support and scholarships) and academically (by redesigning its curriculum to fit ethnic realitites).

- Commit to *preparing* students in math, science, and pre-medical studies.
- Put students on a *clear graduate-degree track* so that very early (in middle and high school) they begin to be acculturated to think in terms of earning four-year degrees, graduate degrees, M.B.A.s, doctorates, and postdoctoral research fellowships and grants.
- Teach students how to *think*, write, and read critically—as well as how to study.
- *Reach out* to the business and professional communities to enlist community leaders as mentors to minority students.
- Hire *faculty totally committed* to changing the lives of minority students, regardless of their ethnicity. (An Anglo committed to this idea is better than, say, a Latino not committed to it. Preferably these teachers will know the culture and the language—will themselves be bicultural.)
- *Encourage* parents to become active participants in school affairs.

In seconding what Robert says, I've added some suggestions of my own:

- Educators should get to know Latinos and the Latino community through more frequent parent-teacher-student meetings both in schools and in Latino neighborhoods. Educators at all levels need to know the minds of Latino children. Their dreams and expectations are different from Anglos', and they cannot be taught without an understanding of their makeup.
- School administrators at all levels must sensitize their personnel to the cultural differences between the Latino and Anglo communities. This means how-to seminars and hands-on supervision. Unless the nuances are mastered, many Latinos will feel misunderstood, and schools and schooling will remain "foreign."
- Teachers should talk to Latinos in small groups on Latino turf. We need to feel comfortable in expressing our views, and this is the best way to effect that. The teacher can bring

back to the actual classroom the ideas, complaints, or visions expressed in the more intimate setting. "I think the class needs to hear what you said last night" is a good way to start a discussion.

- High schools, colleges, and universities should rely more on Latino guest lecturers. Latinos in the sciences, arts, business, and education are superb sources of information and inspiration. And believe me, they'll be delighted to come! I know of no successful Latino who does not wish to share his good fortune with the next generation.

- There is a particular need for more sensitivity to girls. At home too often they're trained to sit by and listen; in class they may follow this pattern even if they have something special to say. The more a girl is called on to speak up in class, either to display her knowledge or share her feelings, the easier it will be for her the next time.

- Students must be encouraged to retain what they learn. Indeed, *encourage* is the right word, for encouragement is a staple of all good teaching (and all good business management). The student who is praised will want more praise; the student who is disparaged will give up. Most of the encouragement will of course be verbal, from teacher to student or peer to student, but prizes (medals, scholarships, and the like) should be given as often as possible. Good students should be asked to participate in outreach programs. Their words will often attract more converts than an administrator's or teacher's. The Latino community lacks role-models for our students. Schools and educators must bring them where we live so they can be publicly lauded and we can be made to understand the extent of their accomplishments. Perhaps they will not garner as much fame as athletes and entertainers, but they will still be recognized as heroes.

I sense that Latino parents who may not have a high school education or are not fluent in English look at schools with a kind of awe, even a kind of fear, and are reluctant to approach them. Similarly, administrators and teachers not brought up in Latino communities may look at those communities as foreign countries, somehow threatening or incomprehensible. That is why dialogue is so vital. Both parties *must* make the effort—for the sake of our kids and our nation.

↬

It is true, as President Clinton is fond of pointing out, that the strength of the United States lies in the diversity of its population. Latinos, as much as any other cultural group, have much to add to the variety and richness of American thought. That such diversity is good for business, too, will be demonstrated in later chapters.

More and more, colleges and universities understand that cross-culturalism is essential to America's lifeblood, and they have begun to woo the Latino community not only with outreach programs but providing courses strictly geared to Latino students. Hispanic groups have been formed and encouraged on a number of campuses, a further means of changing exclusion to inclusion, to make Latinos feel welcome and secure in this "foreign" landscape.

The following list of the top twenty-five colleges for Hispanics in 1996 was compiled by *Hispanic Magazine*, a unique and most welcome example of community outreach. Let's hope the competition among other schools to join the top twenty-five becomes fierce.

- **Arizona State University.** Nine percent of its approximately 30,000 students are Hispanic. One fourth of all degrees are in the fields of business and marketing. There is an active Chicano/Hispanic student coalition which sponsors an annual Culture Week.
- **California State University–Los Angeles.** Even though California has dropped affirmative action as a policy, nearly half the students at Cal State–L.A. are Hispanic. The school boasts outstanding programs in Chicano Studies and has a variety of undergraduate Hispanic organizations.
- **Columbia University.** Nine percent Hispanic, Columbia has the advantage (and disadvantage) of being located in New

York City. It is one of the great universities of the country, and features an outstanding undergraduate and graduate business program. The tuition is high.

- **Florida International University.** Its low in-state tuition makes it particularly attractive for Hispanic students who live in Florida, and they comprise fifty-two percent of the student body. No school in the country graduates more Hispanics with bachelor's or master's degrees.

- **Harvard University.** The oldest (and, many feel, the best) university in America, Harvard's student body is seven percent Hispanic, and most of the recruiting is done by the students themselves—with the administration's active endorsement. Of particular note is the David Rockefeller Center for Latin American Studies.

- **Massachusetts Institute of Technology.** Nine percent Hispanic, this is one of the toughest schools in the country, world-renowned for its science and engineering departments. Its Society of Hispanic Professional Engineers provides student-to-student support and helps members find summer jobs.

- **New Mexico Institute of Mining and Technology.** This small school not only actively recruits Hispanics (nineteen percent of enrollment) but provides them with plenty of student support. Rigorous in math and science—and affordable!

- **New Mexico State University.** Important departments include the Center for Latin American Studies, the Chile Institute, and the Latin American and Caribbean Food Security Movement. The acclaimed Border Research Institute gathers and disseminates information pertaining to Mexico and the Western United States. Students are thirty-five percent Hispanic.

- **New York University.** The program in Ethnic Studies is one of the largest in the country. NYU students (eight percent Hispanic) gain the cultural advantages of New York, a city with two million Puerto Rican inhabitants.

- **Rice University.** Ten percent Hispanic, this excellent private university in Houston has departments of English as a

Second Language and Hispanic and Classical Studies, as well as a number of Hispanic organizations.

- **Rutgers University.** Known for its excellence in the arts and sciences, this great university reflects the cultural diversity of its home state, New Jersey, with eight percent Hispanic enrollment.
- **San Diego State University.** With a strong history of graduating Hispanic students (twenty percent of student body), SDSU not only is affordable but has an excellent outreach program. It puts a special emphasis on U.S./Mexico border relations.
- **Stanford University.** One of the most competitive and prestigious schools in the country, Stanford has made an active effort to increase its Hispanic enrollment, which stands at ten percent. El Centro Chicano operates a student-run cultural center.
- **St. Edward's University.** A small Catholic school in Austin, it was the first university to create a special program for the children of migrant farm workers. Its CAMP program has been widely praised for affording higher education to those who would not otherwise have the opportunity. It is twenty-eight percent Hispanic.
- **St. Mary's University of San Antonio.** Another small Catholic Texas institution, it has been the starting point for numerous Hispanic doctors and lawyers. It ranks among the top thirty in graduating Hispanics, who make up sixty-three percent of the student body.
- **Texas A&M University.** A large university in a rural setting, it is unsurpassed in its engineering and agriculture departments. It has recently been working actively to increase its minority enrollment, now ten percent Hispanic.
- **University of Arizona.** Hispanic enrollment increased by a quarter from 1994 to 1995 and now makes up fourteen percent of the student body. Outreach efforts include the New Start/Summer Bridge Program and the Office of Student Affairs tutoring program.
- **University of California–Berkeley.** With the end of affirma-

tive action, this school made diversity part of the "Berkeley Pledge," and actively recruits. It has thirteen percent Hispanic enrollment and a superb Chicano Studies program.

- **University of California–Los Angeles.** Sixteen percent Hispanic, UCLA is excellent in the fields of business and films. It has a number of Latino and Latin American programs, and numerous official Hispanic student organizations.
- **University of Colorado at Boulder.** CU, with six percent Hispanic students, has recently adopted innovative diversity programs and is striving hard to make all minorities welcome. There are not many more beautiful places to go to school.
- **University of Illinois at Chicago.** UIC has demonstrated its commitment to diversity through the creation of the Latin American Recruitment and Educational Services, whose goal is to assist with the recruiting, enrollment, *and retention* of Hispanic students, who now comprise seventeen percent. This large school in a large city has an excellent academic record.
- **University of Miami.** One quarter Hispanic, it has always had strong ties to the Latino community and ranks high in graduating Hispanic students. Many student organizations are designed specifically to help Hispanic students.
- **University of Texas at Austin.** Here the percentage of Hispanic enrollment has doubled in the last decade and is now at fifteen percent. The school has an excellent combination of high academic standards and affordability and boasts many Hispanic centers and student organizations.
- **University of Texas at El Paso.** Because two-thirds of its student body is Hispanic, UTEP has a history of meeting the particular needs of minority students. It is excellent in engineering and the sciences.
- **University of Texas–Pan American.** Eighty-nine percent Hispanic, this branch located forty miles from the South Texas coast has the most affordable in-state tuition, and its academic standards are improving yearly.

To Ford's Top 25, I add my favorite, not just because my friend Lou Agnese is President, but because I've seen firsthand the great job it does:

- **University of the Incarnate Word.** One of the fastest growing small Catholic universities in the U.S., UIW, located in San Antonio, Texas, focuses on producing successful Hispanic graduates. Its student body reflects the city's majority Hispanic population.

This list was quite different in 1995, proving that many schools are "on the lip" of being included. All major universities have Latino clubs and Latino outreach programs, and their Latino alumni have outreach programs as well in virtually every community. Call the admissions or alumni office at the school you want to attend. They'll help with contacts and give scholarship advice. *Hispanic* magazine also lists the organizations that can help Latinos in their quest for scholarships:

American G.I. Forum of the U.S. Scholarship Fund
2711 W. Anderson Lane, Suite 205
Austin, TX 78757
(512) 392-3025

College Board National Hispanic Scholar Recognition Program
1717 Massachusetts Avenue, N.W.
Suite 401
Washington, DC 20036-2093
(202) 332-7134

Hispanic Association of Colleges and Universities (HACU)
Student Support Systems
4204 Gardendale St. #216
San Antonio, TX 78229
(210) 692-3805

Latin American Professional Women's Foundation
P.O. Box 31532
Los Angeles, CA 90031

League of United Latin American Citizens (LULAC) National
Educational Services (LNESC)
777 N. Capitol Street, S.E. #395
Washington, DC 20002
(202) 408-0060

Lowrider Magazine Scholarship Fund
P.O. Box 648
Walnut, CA 91788-0648
(909) 598-2300

McDonald's Hispanic American Commitment to Education
(HACER) Programs
Contact your high school guidance counselor, local McDonald's
manager, or the National Hispanic Scholarship Fund at (415)
892-9971

Mexican-American Women's National Association (MANA)
Raquel Marquez Frankel Scholarship
1101 17th Street, N.W. #803
Washington, DC 20036-4794
(202) 833-0050

National Hispanic Scholarship Fund
P.O. Box 728
Novato, CA 94948
(415) 892-9971

U.S. Hispanic Chamber of Commerce
1030 15th Street, N.W. #296
Washington, DC 20005
(202) 842-1212

Among the universities on the Ford list, several (Arizona State,
Columbia, Harvard, and others) feature business courses, and
there are of course graduate business schools across the country
that teach the principles and techniques of business practice. My

own feeling is that the best business education you can get is being *in* business itself, but there's no question that an M.B.A. is a practical tool both for getting a job and operating effectively in that job once it's been attained. And a Latino with an M.B.A. makes an ideal "catch" for any corporation. Even if you go into business without a postgraduate degree, many corporations send their employees to business school once they feel the employee is worth the investment.

But business education, of course, starts long before college, with the interaction between parent and child. If you teach your children to work hard, to be fair, to be honest, to fight for what they believe in, and to respect others (including their "different-ness"), then you will have set them on the right road, no matter what the level of their youthful abilities at negotiation or marketing may be. And it is initially from our parents that we learn the most fundamental of business skills: the art of communication.

CHAPTER 8

WHAT YOU SAY ISN'T WHAT YOU MEAN

El arte de la comunicación

Good business relies on clear communication. Unless each party knows what the other means, there is the danger of ambiguity, the probability of its attendant loss of faith, and the real chance of failure.

So it is essential for Latinos dealing with Anglo businesses to speak the same language. By this I don't mean just being fluent in the language of business—English. I mean understanding those subtleties that are part of any communication, things that are implied or left unsaid, a kind of code that can be learned only by acute observation and practice.

Most Latinos living in the United States are bilingual and bi-cultural, great assets in a world where more and more corporations are becoming committed to doing business with Latin America. If you are fluent in Spanish, you can learn other Latin-based languages—French, Italian, Portuguese—with relative ease. *No hay problema.* And then your opportunities in a global economy where worldwide trade is the norm are virtually limitless.

Most Anglos, by contrast, speak only English and have

difficulty with foreign languages. In fact, many times Anglo Americans actually *expect* the rest of the world to learn English, so they don't have to bother with other languages. Many also have difficulties with foreign cultures. So it makes sense that they will rely on Latinos more and more to be part of their team when it comes to doing business with Latin countries and—by extension—for doing business, period. We are therefore a vital link in a new world economy.

Language is a tricky commodity. We as Latinos must be careful how we use it to communicate with Anglos, just as we must be sure they are equally understanding when it comes to communicating with us.

Mexicans, Puerto Ricans, and Central Americans tend to be more subservient in their language—and in their demeanor—than Latinos from Spain or Cuba. The more Spanish or European the country's population is, the less subservient the language will be in its daily use. In Brazil, Argentina, Uruguay, Chile, Paraguay, and Venezuela the indigenous Indians were practically annihilated by the Spanish and Portuguese, so the *conquistador* or "boss" mentality prevails; Cuba is the Caribbean example of this. In places where the indigenous population survived—in Mexico, Panama, Guatemala, El Salvador, Costa Rica, the northern cone of South America, and the high Andean mountains of Bolivia— you will find a much more submissive attitude in the Spanish language.

It is important to be aware of the differences. For example, say "thank you" and the Anglo response is "you're welcome." In South America or Cuba, the response will probably be *"encantado"* (charmed), but the Mexican and Central American response is *"para servirle"* (I'm here to serve you) or *"de nada"* (it's nothing)—replies that say volumes about the way language can make us appear subservient.

These are subtle differences, reflecting how the language is used from day to day in common practice. *"Para servirle"* and *"de nada"* appear in all Latin languages, French and Italian included, but the usage varies in equally subtle ways. It's not enough, therefore, to master the vocabulary and grammar of the language; one must master the nuances as well. One must be careful to precisely understand not only what is being said but what implications lie underneath the words.

For example, look at this "miscommunications" chart:

Phrase	Literal Translation	Meaning to Latino	Implication to Anglo
Para servirle	Here to serve you	My pleasure	Wow! My valet!
De nada	It's nothing	You're welcome	He/she must believe what I'm saying "thanks" for has little value
Mándeme (response after name is called)	Command me	Yes?	He/she must want me to tell him/her what to do
¿En qué le puedo servir?	How may I serve you?	How can I help you?	He/she wants to *serve* me
No sé de esas cosas (common response to complicated question)	I don't know about such things	It's not my place to have an opinion	Not a very smart person
Así lo quiere Dios (response to bad luck or unmet goals)	That's the way God wants it	It's not so bad; what could I expect?	This person has no initiative
Nos vemos a las seis para cenar (making a dinner date)	See you at six for dinner	I'll see you somewhere between 6:15 and 6:30, maybe 7:00	He's/she's late— but then, he's/she's always late
Mañana paso a recoger el paquete	I'll pick up the package tomorrow	I'll pick up the package first chance I get	He/she didn't pick it up— how undependable

You'll rarely find a Mexican calling his boss by his first name, whereas the former chairman of the Times Mirror Corporation walked into a meeting I attended with the words, "Call me Al." The former implies a *patrón/peón* mind-set, the other, true or not, a relationship of colleagues.

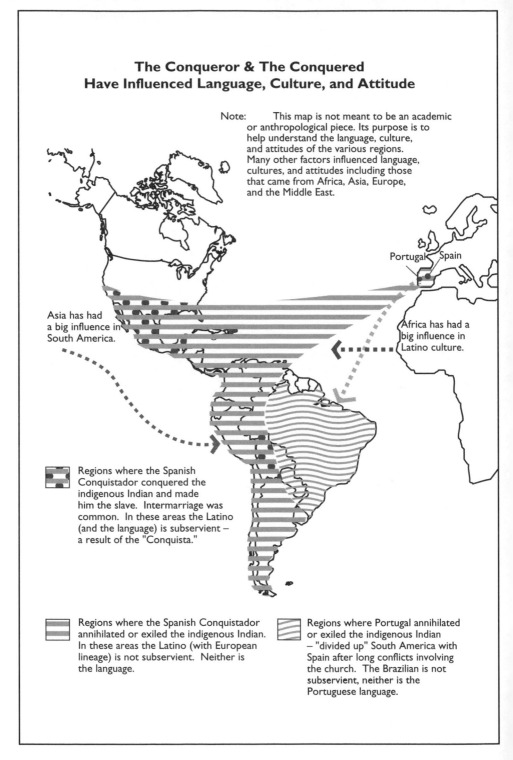

The Conqueror & The Conquered
Have Influenced Language, Culture, and Attitude

Note: This map is not meant to be an academic or anthropological piece. Its purpose is to help understand the language, culture, and attitudes of the various regions. Many other factors influenced language, cultures, and attitudes including those that came from Africa, Asia, Europe, and the Middle East.

Portugal Spain

Asia has had a big influence in South America.

Africa has had a big influence in Latino culture.

Regions where the Spanish Conquistador conquered the indigenous Indian and made him the slave. Intermarriage was common. In these areas the Latino (and the language) is subservient — a result of the "Conquista."

Regions where the Spanish Conquistador annihilated or exiled the indigenous Indian. In these areas the Latino (with European lineage) is not subservient. Neither is the language.

Regions where Portugal annihilated or exiled the indigenous Indian — "divided up" South America with Spain after long conflicts involving the church. The Brazilian is not subservient, neither is the Portuguese language.

Many Latinos don't have a grasp of idiom, and therefore what to them seems appropriate might dismay their Anglo listeners. Take this lyric from an old but newly popular song, *"La media vuelta"* ("The Half-Turn," as in "I'm turning halfway round to walk away from you"), as an example:

> *Te vas porque yo quiero que te vayas,*
> *A la hora que yo quiera te detengo.*
> *Yo sé que mi cariño te hace falta,*
> *Aunque quieras o no, yo soy tu dueño.*

> You're leaving 'cause I *want* you to leave.
> At whatever time I wish, you'll return.
> I know you need my loving—
> And like it or not, *I'm* your master.

What could be more chauvinistic? Yet the words are passionately beautiful in Spanish and I've seen young women today swoon, as they hear Luis Miguel croon the lyrics. Talking tough is for us—man or woman—a way of declaring love and is not to be taken literally. If the song were played here in translation, Luisito would be run out of town.

∽

Since so many of us have been brought up to follow rather than to lead, to serve rather than *be* served, our subservience is apparent not only in our language but in our bearing.

Recently we bought a new home. Kathy and I planned to use the top floor for living quarters, and the KJS offices were to occupy the downstairs. All this entailed a good deal of renovation, and we consulted an architect who in turn hired a team of young, energetic Mexicans (legal? who knows?) to do the actual construction work. With this book in mind, I watched them carefully.

The workers were diligent and intelligent, yet they never questioned their boss or me, even when we gave conflicting orders. When they spoke to me, they would remove their hats but rarely make eye contact. They backed away when I said hello, as though

I were about to criticize them, though they were responsible only to their foreman. I sensed that because I earn a higher income than they did, they considered me more knowledgeable in matters of construction, even though I knew nothing about it. They came early, stayed late, and worked weekends. I knew they were being paid little, even though it was the going wage; their body language said "use me, abuse me."

Their attitude reminded me of a different "construction" job I had commissioned a few years earlier. I had bought a 1940 Lincoln with the idea of getting it restored. I love old cars, and often do the restoration work myself locally, employing a good friend from Mexico who does very decent work. But this time the job was too extensive, so I took it to the best restoration company in Texas, a hundred miles away. The craftsmen were German, and Michael, the owner, told me, "Here we refurbish cars until they are the equivalent of Rembrandts and Renoirs." He promised delivery in six months and quoted a very high price, but I was impressed by his confidence and agreed.

Two years later the job was finished. It wound up costing me *four times* what I had agreed to pay, but once the work started, I had to complete it, and when I saw the finished automobile, the cost was worth it. It *was* a Rembrandt—I treasure it.

The point here is that Mike and his team of craftsmen made me share their confidence. It was not so much what they said but their pride, their demeanor, and their assurance. "We are the only ones for the job," their manner implied. "Of course you can back out, but to whom would you turn? You asked for the best. We're giving you the best. We're sorry it's taking longer and costing more, but old cars are tricky. You'll be happy when the job's finished. Just wait."

By contrast, my friend from Mexico, Pedro Chavez, has restored a Volkswagen bug and a Karmann Ghia for two of my kids. He always does good work, but his attitude is quite different from Mike's. He smiles. He bows. He cuts corners when he can. And he charges a lot less than he could.

I value Pedro as much as I value Mike. Certainly each person fills a niche and a need. Nevertheless, I wonder how much more Pedro could earn with his own talent and Mike's attitude.

⤳

Confidence is the bedrock of business communication, and it is not easy to master; it can come only when you're sure of your own work and your own abilities. And it's particularly difficult when dealing with Anglos, since it means learning a new way of communicating, one that understands what lies behind what we say and feel and recognizes that Anglos think and feel in different ways.

I've learned a lot about those differences through my work in advertising. If you are to communicate with and sell a product or service to a Latino audience, you must appeal primarily to their emotions—*tienes que llegarle al corazón.* If you sell to an Anglo audience, you must appeal to reason as well as (or instead of) the heart.

Ads for McDonald's, which stress the emotional world of family values over the "benefit" of good food at a low price, are particularly effective in a Latino market; "you deserve a break today" also has a particular resonance. So are ads for Coke (world harmony over the "benefit" of refreshment), Kodak (happy memories over clear pictures), Nike (personal achievement over performance), and Hallmark ("care enough to send the very best" over an easy way to convey greetings). I've found that the number two brands in each case simply don't tug as hard at the heartstrings, which may explain *why* they're number two. The less soulful approach may work fine for the Anglo market, but it doesn't work among Hispanics. Burger King will not beat "family values"; Pepsi cannot top "world harmony." If you want to communicate effectively to a Latino audience, you have no choice. You *must* communicate with the emotions.

Some companies produce different commercials for the different markets. To Anglos, for example, Western Union stresses that their service is the fastest way to send money. To Hispanics, however, many of whom wire money to their relatives in Latin America on a regular basis, the appeal is "we're here to help you keep your promise"—that is, the promise you made to take care of your family when you earned your fortune in America.

There are other examples. To Anglos, Columbia Health Care

stresses its ability to deliver "quality health care at a good price." To Hispanics, the same company becomes the "protector of life." And for the San Antonio Water System, we chose to emphasize much more than their ability to provide high quality water anytime it was needed. To Hispanics, we must communicate to the heart—let them know that water nurtures life, that water in fact *is* life. The company's logo is a long-haired goddess holding an earthen bowl into which rain from the heavens is pouring.

The Texas water appeal is particularly interesting because it so directly relates the product to God. Yet in all the emotional appeals, there is an attempt to give a kind of Godlike aura to the product. Coke is like God; it gives the subtle message that it is the "real thing." McDonald's is like God; it promotes the family virtues stressed in the Bible. What we're dealing with here is the logic of the heart, not the logic of reason, and the power of its effect on everyone, but especially Latinos, is remarkable.

You can see this emotional strain in all aspects of Latino life. Physically, we touch each other more than Anglos do. A greeting between men combines a handshake with an *abrazo*. Men often walk arm in arm down the street in Spain and Latin America; women do it routinely. Like our homelands we are lush and warm. We are extraordinarily open with each other. We communicate through a touch, a gesture, an embrace, but often leave unsaid what our deepest feelings are, partly for fear of hurting or embarrassing someone, including ourselves.

All these communication nuances have tremendous ramifications when it comes to the world of business. We've seen that Latinos are reluctant to express their opinions openly or say what they really feel, and in focus groups we've had to analyze body language to learn their true feelings. This is a trait inherited from our ancestors—the slave has no feelings, no opinions. Latinos are also accustomed to indirection. We're loath to criticize overtly, for example, no matter how much we dislike a person or product. We rely heavily on the listener to glean our honest appraisals through a thicket of gesture, innuendo, and nuance. *"Tú sabes;*

no tengo que explicar"—you know what I mean; I don't have to explain.

Mark McCormack, the author of *What They Didn't Teach You at Harvard Business School,* says that business relationships are really developed in the casual conversations before, during, and after the official business meeting. Business, he points out, like everything else, relies on personal relationships—it's people to people, how you feel about each other, how much you like each other, how much you trust each other. Learning to be more open and more free with our opinions and with our feelings, sharing those intimacies that help develop deep, long-lasting relationships often means the difference between success and super-success.

Anglo business works at a speed that dazzles many Latinos. Personal relationships are critical, but trust is often established in a single meeting. In Latin America, businesspeople tend to rely on two, three, five or more "premeetings" (including meals, social evenings, family get-togethers) before business is approached. "Let's get down to business" is a familiar Anglo phrase, generally uttered even at a first-time meeting after just a few minutes of small talk. The Anglo approach is usually direct, "no-nonsense." Many times, the bonding essential to any relationship is established at a slow pace. Here's where the Latino is at an advantage. We don't put the deal first and the personal relationship later. We enjoy both, and that leads to long friendships and long-lasting business. All we have to do is take McCormack's advice and do our bonding in between meetings, not make it the meeting itself.

Unaccustomed to speaking directly, used to a different kind of bonding, favoring nuance over a straight-out approach, we sometimes find ourselves bewildered when dealing with Anglos. Of course! We're dealing in a foreign business culture, playing by someone else's rules. The "gringo" rules.

Think about it. The transition from long-term to short-term bonding should not be too difficult for us. Our warmth and desire to be close, to please, are perfect traits. Our social skills are well known and appreciated among Anglos. But somehow at the very times when we should be most comfortable, we freeze. The DNA that should make us easily accessible to strangers shorts out into a hesitancy and awkwardness—a sense of not belonging, perhaps—that makes dealing with Anglos far more difficult than it should be. We stammer even when we're sure of our position. We avoid eye contact. We're brusque, seemingly anxious for the meeting to end, for the "torture" to cease.

Perhaps we're uncomfortable precisely because, despite all our similarities as human beings and mutuality of business goals, we can see that in some important way Anglos *are* different. So our behavior is not surprising. Who isn't hesitant when facing the unknown?

Here's what I recommend: Think of the Anglo as a Latino, and regard him or her as such. Instead of Andy Kelly he's Andres Gonzales; instead of Sally Rogers she's Sandra Rodriguez. Andres and Sandra live in your neighborhood. They have families, pets, fears, strengths, emotions just like you. Indeed, they're already your friends. *"Ya somos amigos, nos conocemos"*—we know each other as friends.

Try this the next time you do business with an Anglo. It will be hard at first, but you'll be amazed how avidly the Anglo will respond to your approach. It's the way Anglos approach each other, as though they already know each other. To Anglos it's not only recognizable, it's the only approach they're accustomed to. You'll see them relax—you're on Anglo turf. If they experience an initial sense of discomfort (after all, you're "different" too) it will soon ease, even as yours does.

Your comfort level will rise, the atmosphere of strangeness will begin to evaporate, and you may even find yourself hoping the meeting will go on. If there are family pictures on the desk, talk of your own family. If it's clear you both like baseball, talk of Roberto Alomar, Chipper Jones, or Rey Ordoñez. Here, you're talking baseball, not necessarily Hispanic. These need not be long conversations—as I say, the Anglo wants to get down to business—but they'll introduce a commonality to the relationship, one that will grow if your mutual business arrangement succeeds.

⌐

It is a truism that in order to hear what the other person is saying we have to *listen*. Yet sometimes, in our haste to "get it over with," we don't really listen, or we jump to conclusions and mistakenly say what we think the Anglo wants to hear in response.

Recently we were pitching our agency to a prospective client, eager to get his business. A young account executive from our team had established the initial contact with the prospect, and I let her run the meeting.

"There are three things we want from any advertising agency," the prospect's vice president of marketing declared.

"I know," our young executive said. "Service, service, service."

"No," said the VP. "The first thing is trust. The second thing is—"

"Service."

"No, the second thing is creativity. The third thing is . . ."

"Service!" she shouted. "I've got to be right this time."

The VP looked at her with amusement and smiled. "Price."

"Oops. I get it," she said, red-faced.

I tell the anecdote not to put down the young woman. In fact, her enthusiasm paid off; we won the business. She quickly learned to improve her responses and went on to acquire a lot of business for our agency. But I tell it to point out that in our desire to serve— *"para servirle"*—we don't always listen, and in our anxiety to get the job, we may jump in before we're exactly sure what the job is.

Of course service is important, but there's more. The young executive leaped to a conclusion based on her own culture and background. She did not stop to realize that the VP's culture and background were different. He took service for granted; he was interested in the other things.

My executive fell into the *peón* category of Latino business types. The *patrón* makes equally large but quite different mistakes.

Patrones have preconceived ideas of their role: protector, problem solver, the ultimate expert. *"En esta casa yo mando"* (in this house, I rule) is their motto. Their self-assurance, confidence, positiveness, aggressiveness, and sense of entitlement are all fine qualities *in moderation*, but they can blind the *patrón* to the needs and wishes of others.

Here's an example from a friend's personal life:

Antonio Castillo and his wife, Nancy, an Anglo, had been married for eighteen years. Outwardly they were the perfect couple, and their three teenagers were all doing well in school and had their parents' social ease and charm. I would have sworn that nothing could break up this family; the marriage, I was sure, would last another fifty years.

One day Antonio came to me ashen-faced. "Nancy's left me."

I was stunned. "Why?"

"She said she doesn't love me anymore."

"I see."

"No. You don't. Of course she loves me. There has to be something else. 'What's the real reason?' I asked her."

"What did she say?"

"She repeated that she didn't love me. I told her to be real, to tell me the truth. I asked again: 'What's the *real* reason?' "

"And—?"

"She just said she didn't love me anymore." He shook his head disconsolately. "I don't understand. Why won't she level with me?"

"Antonio," I said, "you're not listening. Maybe she *doesn't* love you anymore. Go back and ask her why she feels the way she does."

Tony was furious. "You don't get it, do you? She loves me! She's just not telling the truth."

Poor Antonio. He had simply stopped listening to his wife. He ruled his family with too strong a hand. All the decisions were his; Nancy had little say and less freedom. Eventually she got fed up with it. The deep love she initially felt faded under his rule. She told him that. He didn't want to hear. And so she left.

As in marriage, so in business. Communication does not mean command, it means a back-and-forth, a sharing of ideas, a willingness to hear another's viewpoint and to make an all-out effort to understand it. Teamwork and trust are the essence of all good business, meaning partnership, not patronage.

And as in business, so in politics. Perhaps my best lesson in understanding the importance of the ability to listen and share ideas came from Senator John Tower in 1978, when I was in charge of his campaign in Texas for the Hispanic community. Tower knew how desperately he needed a large Hispanic vote to win. He understood and appreciated the Latinos. He admired their work ethic, endorsed their family values, loved America with a passion equal to theirs—and shared their taste for Lone Star Beer.

"Lionel," he'd say to me after a day of hard campaigning, "it's six o'clock. Let's find some folks to talk to." And so we'd go to a few Hispanic "ice houses," where we'd sit at picnic tables with the workmen— *"Buenas tardes, soy John Tower"*—and swap political stories (he knew all the good ones) and opinions. He *enjoyed* these conversations, and his pleasure rubbed off on the customers (that is, voters), who almost certainly went home to tell their families what a swell guy Tower was. Tower was just as comfortable with Republican bigwigs whose money and endorsement he needed, but I was more struck with his communication with *my* people. He won their respect and trust, and in so doing won the election. If *anyone* knows how to communicate, it's a good politician.

If we as businesspeople think as Tower did ("I'm going to win them over—these Anglo businesspeople; I'll win their respect and trust as well"), we'll be welcomed as Tower was by the Hispanic voters. We must put ourselves in their suits, try to understand their mind-set and their concerns. And the more we're able to put ourselves among Anglo businesspeople, the easier the communication.

⌇

About one out of five Latinos in this country are married to Anglos; I am one of them. And the number is sure to grow. If Latinos and Anglos can fall in love, unquestionably they can do business together, and indeed my marriage to Kathy has made me feel more relaxed and confident in "gringo" social and business situations, just as she is more relaxed and confident among Latinos.

The more we learn about each other, the more we will recognize our similarities; thus our differences will seem less strange. Profitable business communication between Latinos and Anglos rests on

- Confidence in ourselves as people, as professionals
- A willingness to listen and to understand

- The ability to entertain a point of view other than our own
- A facility for speaking openly and honestly
- A desire to get into the consumer's or client's mind
- The knowledge that we are everyone's equal, and that everyone is equal to us

It is this last that brings us to the next chapter. For if you are as good as anybody else, and can become anyone else's colleague, you have the ability to network.

CHAPTER 9

NETWORKING

Entre amigos

At the Franklin Delano Roosevelt Library in Hyde Park, New York, there is a series of fascinating letters Franklin wrote to his mother when he was in grade school. In them he talks about his classmates, the children of important families. ("Today I met so-and-so. His father is the Senator from Massachusetts. I need to get to know him better.")

I'm sure he wrote the letters primarily to please his mother; it's unlikely a child that young would "network." But they reveal how even in grade school he was being taught that relationships were an important instrument for advancement. His mother knew it. Franklin learned quickly. And as an adult Roosevelt became the *master* networker, *un hombre que se mueve bien,* the model for another president who used networking as a prime political tool—Lyndon Johnson.

There are dozens of pictures of Congressman Johnson standing as close as possible to Roosevelt; the viewer was patently meant to assume the two were confidants. Later there are thousands of pictures of President Johnson, arm around another politician's shoulder. The body language suggests networking; Johnson was using his own influence, carefully built through the years, to induce his colleagues to support his pet projects.

I had a firsthand look at political networking when I was one of a group of Texas businesspeople invited to Washington by President Clinton to work for passage of the North American Free Trade Alliance (NAFTA) treaty. Delegations of businesspeople from every state gathered at the Museum of American History. Each delegation in turn met with President Clinton, who chatted with us informally about a variety of business topics. He seemed to be enjoying himself, and his pleasure rubbed off on us, so that by the time he got to what he wanted—we were to lobby our congressmen to vote for the treaty—we were solidly on his side.

Clinton knew precisely which congressmen were unalterably opposed to the treaty and which had already guaranteed their sponsorship. *Lo tenía todo en la cabeza*—he knew the details by heart. Our job was to go after the undecided, and we set about our task with fervor. I left Washington convinced that the treaty would pass, and deeply impressed by Clinton's performance. He had used his powers of persuasion (helped by the power of the presidency itself, a potent force one-on-one) to foster passage of something he believed in. He had motivated us through friendship and personal interaction to do his bidding.

Clinton's behavior, like Roosevelt's and Johnson's, may seem calculated, even ungenuine. Some people wouldn't consider engaging in such open networking. But I think they feel that way because they don't understand networking's benefits. Networking is more than getting to know someone who can later help your business. It is a way of helping one another.

Most networking depends on openness, not being devious, doing good for someone without directly expecting the favor repaid. The best networkers are by nature outgoing, friendly, socially adept, interested less in themselves than in others, conscious not so much of how people might help them as how they might help people.

Networking starts in the family. Never be too proud to accept a lead, a contact, a job set up by a family member.

But whether or not your family can help you, most networking is achieved between acquaintances-become-friends, and in this regard everyone you meet can potentially be of assistance. Indeed my motto about networking is this: *una manera de ayudarnos unos a otros*—just a way of helping each other.

Much networking takes place early in life, at school. Lou Agnese says that the main difference between going to a "top 25" school and a "regular" college is not so much the level of education (although there's a difference) as it is the quality of the classmates you meet. At Harvard or Yale, students have what he describes as a "super success mentality," and if you are "one of them" or *friends* with one of them, when they succeed they will help you succeed. Most times a job will go to a college (or high school) classmate over an equally qualified (or even more qualified) stranger. It's networking through friendships and it's how business operates—*una realidad de los negocios.*

Patently, few Latinos go to Ivy League schools (though the number is growing), but the principle applies everywhere: if you become friends with people before they're successful, they'll help you once they achieve success.

So start early. Be nice to everyone. The more sensitive you are to others' feelings and wishes, the more likely it is that you'll be repaid in the future. I'm not advocating a "put-on sensitivity"; it must be genuine. Empathy can be learned, the ability to put yourself in another's place can be cultivated so that soon it becomes natural. Learn to listen to what lies underneath words that are often halting. Overcome shyness through practice. Put yourself out for everyone even if there seems to be no immediate quid pro quo.

When I was a young man, I had a discussion with an even younger man about advertising. I was already established; he was considering the profession as his career choice. I quickly forgot the conversation, but twenty years later, he called me to introduce me to the director of marketing at the Brown & Williamson Tobacco Corporation, his client, who was looking for a new advertising agency for his company. My long-ago acquaintance, who had decided to accept a position in Chicago at Campbell-Mithun advertising, now led me through the tortuous maze of competing for the firm's business. A number of presentations were required, and my newly discovered sponsor critiqued each of mine, telling me what to say and what not to say the next time. Without his help, I would not have landed the account. With it, I won out. The job was worth nine million dollars to our new agency, in effect helping us get started by easing the financial pressures that afflict any new firm, large or small.

And I won the business because I was once nice to a young man who wanted advice (thirty minutes' worth!) and throughout two decades remembered.

⤳

Perhaps the best networker I know is Ron Meraz, whom I recently met in southern California. Ron is a stockbroker with Merrill Lynch, and for the first few years of his business life he did what most stockbrokers do: he made calls to strangers, asking for their business.

Because of his skill as a salesman, he was able to build a fairly good list of clients (working for a prominent firm didn't hurt either), but he was dissatisfied. Then he hit on his goal. "I wanted to build wealth for my own people," he told me. *"Quería ayudar a mi gente.* I wanted to be the first broker to do business primarily with Latinos."

Knowing that on the whole Latinos are a cautious lot, Ron assumed that banks would have a number of Latino customers who had $100,000 or more in savings accounts, earning only three percent interest. If he could identify them, he thought, he could woo them and win them over to Merrill Lynch. He figured that he would be able to convince them that they could invest in super-safe stocks and bonds and still be able to double their interest income.

But where to find them? Ron turned to his friends. Most did not have enough money saved to invest in the market, but some of them had friends who did, and Ron went after those. At first he devoted about ten percent of his time to searching for Latino investors, but as more and more Latinos agreed to do business with him, he realized the true extent of the market's potential. Now he spends nearly two-thirds of his time in this area.

"It's amazing how many Latinos who are between fifty and seventy years old have been saving all their lives," he said. "Not much at a time—maybe a hundred dollars a month—but over all those years it adds up. And they never *thought* of any place to keep it but in a bank."

Once they began to invest, Ron kept in close touch with them. "They're really the first generation of Latino investors," he told me. "I can't tell you how much I like doing business with my own people. They trust me. They respect me. And once they're in, they refer me to others."

To date, Latinos have entrusted to Ron four hundred million dollars in assets. His goal: one billion! He's doing well now; if he reaches his goal, the commissions will make him a multimillionaire. And all because he asked his Latino friends for help, and those friends called their friends in an ever widening spiral.

That's networking!

⌣

It seems that the more successful you are, the more your ability to network has led to that success. For example:

- After talk-show host Geraldo Rivera lost his job at *20-20* in 1985 (he wanted to do an explosive story on Marilyn Monroe's death; management said no; the resulting dispute culminated in his being fired), he came to San Antonio to be a judge at a tamale cook-off one of our clients had sponsored. He quickly told us of his goal: to start a brand-new type of talk show covering explosive subjects—he called it "dramatic talk television." Over three days, Kathy and I introduced his idea to a number of our clients. They were all aghast. "Too radical," they said and refused to sponsor the show. Yet I watched Geraldo with admiration. He was confident in his presentations, sure that the show would succeed, delighted to use the network we had provided. He struck out in San

Antonio. Back in New York, he struck gold. He helped create a new TV genre.

- Tejano singing star Selena, with whom I worked on commercials for Coca-Cola, was a fabulous networker. A superb businesswoman, she always knew people's names and treated them cordially, no matter what their position. She is remembered at Coke (and everywhere else, for that matter) for her diplomacy, warmth, and consideration. These qualities were equally evident with her fans. She genuinely loved to make people happy, not only with her singing but through personal contact. Her network encompassed literally millions of people, people who continue to be her fans even after her death.

- The actor Edward James Olmos carries a cellular phone with him at all times. But his calls generally do not concern business; those he leaves to his agent. He's passionately involved in working with Hispanic cultural causes, everything from helping the Indians in Chiapas to promoting Hispanic education and scholarships through public service announcements. He spends more time on these concerns than on his acting career—and he uses his celebrity to persuade corporations, other actors, his friends, and friends of his friends to help. He probably does more pro bono work than anyone in the entertainment field. Eddie networks for the love of his people and his community.

- My friend Jesse Trevino is among the best known of Hispanic artists. His paintings sell for twenty-five to forty thousand dollars each (*¡mucho dinero!*), yet I'm convinced that despite his enormous talent he would not receive such high prices without his having carefully established a network of gallery owners, art connoisseurs, and critics to praise his work. He knows the value of publicity; he's a genuinely warm and considerate man; he is not too proud to accept help. Recently a group of his friends bought a large painting of his and donated it to the Smithsonian Institution with the stipulation that it hang there on permanent display. He is the first Hispanic painter to be so honored. And, looking at it recently, I was struck by the thought that the recluse Vincent Van Gogh died in near poverty, while the outgoing Pablo Picasso died a multimillionaire. Coincidence, or the ability and desire to network?

- The CEO of the most successful advertising agency in Colombia is Christian Toro. I've traveled with him and am amazed at his ability to network. He always flies first class, on the theory that he might meet a business executive who will want to hire his agency, and he carries with him a small video recorder so he can show a prospective client his reel of commercials on the spot. I don't have to tell you that he also carries a cellular phone, a pager, a fax machine, and a computer so he can consistently keep up with his other contacts when no immediate prospect is at hand. Christian is truly a twenty-first-century networker. Sometimes Latinos can teach gringos a few tricks.

⤳

But these are famous and powerful people. "*Son diferentes—* they're different," you might think. "I'm just an ordinary person trying to get started. I don't have many contacts. I'm naturally shy. I'm uncomfortable with Anglos. I love your success stories, Lionel, but I live in a different world."

Not so different. Famous people were once unknown; most successful entrepreneurs started with little; every one of us has experienced shyness; all of us are uncomfortable in the presence of "others."

So where do you start?

Let's say fate has brought you to a small city where you know no one. You've landed a job with a manufacturer of auto parts, but your goal of starting your own machine-tool business seems a distant and unattainable dream. You need friends, contacts, companionship. You need a network.

Obviously, the place to start is in the office, where gossip—*el chisme*—soon becomes a valuable networking tool, and your colleagues, Latino and Anglo, will generally be glad to "show you the ropes." But I'd advise, too, that you take an after-hours volunteer job—the Red Cross, the United Way, Meals on Wheels, a museum, a political club.

Hispanic charitable organizations are always looking for volunteers to serve the Hispanic community; offer your services. Join the folklórico group, the local Latino acting group, an organization that deals with kids at risk. Make yourself available for community cleanups, fairs, and cultural festivals. You'll get yourself known, make friends, have fun. And when you least expect it, one of those contacts or friendships will turn into big business.

When you're starting your own business, join business organizations and trade associations, register at the Chamber of Commerce, as well as the Hispanic Chamber of Commerce if there is a local branch. You'll quickly get accepted, get known in the business community, and you'll almost certainly find a colleague happy to give guidance or advice or a business lead.

There are networking opportunities and organizations such as the ones I've noted in every community to welcome people just like you. But for now it's important to know this overriding principle: You must create your own network. It will not come to you.

That means you must be outgoing, sociable, optimistic, aware that most people *want* to welcome you. You have to be able to take the occasional rejection with an increased desire to try again, and you must realize that networking takes time and persistence. Be friendly. Be interested in others. The network will begin to grow.

And remember: The seeds you plant in early life often flower many years later. Plant as many seeds as you can, but don't wait around for them to grow. They will, but sometimes only years later.

∽

You'd think that Latinos would be natural networkers. In the countries where we, our parents, or our grandparents were born, we were taught to fend for ourselves. Without government programs to fall back on, *tenemos poco, pero nos defendemos*—we've had to live by our wits, and rely on our friends and colleagues. Also, our cultural values of family, trust, and community all involve networking, and our natural instincts for friendliness and bargaining ability hone our networking skills.

Yet it's tough for us to network with "them." Anglos, we know, network with other Anglos; most of us see it happen on a daily basis. Why, then, don't we plug into the circuits?

One reason is that we have simply been told too many times to know our place. *"No te adelantes, no seas igualado"*—don't be forward. If it's in our nature to be diffident, to not question authority, to not speak until spoken to, to wait for orders (like the construction men working on my house), then networking with people different from us is next to impossible. Since we must "catch up," we must learn to take the lead, and that means approaching first, speaking first, inviting first, pretending that the Anglo is another Latino *igual como nosotros*—just like us.

Not easy. It's all very well to tell ourselves we're equal to anyone, even if he or she earns more, is better known, or occupies a more powerful position. But that's not the same thing as *feeling* equal, and it's the feeling that counts.

One technique I've used successfully is to think of the powerful Anglo before me as my best high school buddy and to talk to him or her as I would to any close friend. Again, that can be difficult, but if in your mind you replace the Anglo's face with your friend's, and if you repeat the exercise enough, then you'll be surprised at how easy it becomes. And with ease comes comfort, with comfort genuine friendship. Remember: when you can relax, the person you're talking to will also relax.

Successful people ask for help routinely, so don't hesitate in expressing your goals and asking for assistance in obtaining them. And ask straightforwardly. If you call for an appointment to follow up on a conversation you might have had at a cocktail party, for example, you might find it comfortable to say, "I wonder if I might have a moment to talk to Mr. Smith." Instead say, "I'm calling to follow up on a conversation Jim and I had last Tuesday evening. Is he in? No? Can you look at his calendar to see when he has an hour free this week?" Nine times out of ten you'll get your appointment. It's all in your attitude—act as though you expect to get it, and you'll get it.

The telephone, in fact, is still the best instrument for networking there is. Think of it as an ally, and learn to use it correctly. Anglos as well as Latinos find it difficult to pick up the phone to call for a favor, even if the person on the other end is a friend. They find it even more difficult to call a stranger for any purpose, feeling perhaps that they're intruding in that person's activities, that they're being a "bother." This usually comes from an innate sense of unworthiness, and again it can be overcome by practice. And here's a good hint: Make your most difficult or unpleasant calls first thing in the morning, before you make any other. That way the calls won't hang over your head for the entire day, and you'll find the rest of your calls, medium-difficult and not particularly difficult, will come a lot easier as well.

⌣

During my career I've networked both consciously and unconsciously. The longer you do it, the more fruitful each contact gets. The main rule is, don't be shy. Just do it. Network among organizations where few Latinos tread; you may be the only Latino in the group, and you're sure to stand out. Here's a list of suggestions.

Join at least two professional organizations. I recommend:

The local Chamber of Commerce
The Hispanic Chamber of Commerce

Volunteer for at least one community organization. Choose the one that interests you, but make sure other businesspeople who are networking prospects are active in it. Possibilities include:

The United Way
The Salvation Army
The Lions Club
The local LULAC

Volunteer for fund-raising projects, especially capital campaigns such as those for

Junior high or high school building additions
Local college or university libraries
Restoration of old neighborhood "historic landmarks"
Community cultural centers

Join social clubs like

Alumni associations
"Spanish" clubs (you can always learn more)
Cooking or baking or sewing clubs
Choral societies
Reading groups
Toastmasters

Volunteer to serve on boards or committees. You'll be amazed at how many are looking for Latino members. Good bets are:

The United Way (allocations, finance committees, etc.)
Symphony orchestras, choral societies, theater groups, and the
    like
Schools, colleges, and universities
Museums
Nature conservancies

Again, before you join, look over the list of active members of these organizations and make sure they consist of real business prospects.

Fly first class as soon as you can afford it. You'll meet other businesspeople, many in key positions.

Attend mixers. Have a networking goal before you go, anticipate who might be there, initiate conversations. Look for influential people, exchange business cards, tell them about yourself. But don't spend more than ten minutes with any one person at a mixer. Follow up by phone.

Give parties yourself and invite colleagues and the boss.

Pick up the check.

Be particularly nice to students and beginners. It will surprise you how quickly some of them will grow to a position where they'll be able to help you.

Listen, listen, listen. Take notes, remember names, spouses' and children's included.

Don't just phone, write. On personalized stationery, as soon as you can afford it.

    Send follow-up letters
    Send congratulatory notes
    Print and use *Gracias* and *Felicitaciones* cards
    Express sympathy for another's personal misfortune

Keep your office door open. Those who enter will welcome your generosity of spirit and respond with their own.

Don't be "too tired" or "too busy" to consider someone who asks for help. See as many as you can, and help—really help—as many as you can.

Don't be shy to ask for help yourself when you need it.

Don't be reluctant to ask your friends for favors—and let them ask you. That's what friends are for. And when you promise a favor, always do it.

Try to incorporate these hints into your life. The business world is crowded. Remember: others are networking too—both men and women.

CHAPTER 10

THE LATINA WOMAN IS THE BACKBONE OF OUR CULTURE

La fuerza de nuestra cultura

Years ago, when we first conducted research into the minds of young Latino males to determine why they opted to enlist in the army rather than to enter the workforce, I was astounded at the results. We found that in most cases they made the decision in concert with their mom—not their dad, who was strangely absent from the conversation.

More recently, when we were interviewing Hispanic families on their health care, we again found that Mamá, not Papá, makes the critical decisions on what doctors and hospitals and even what insurance to choose. If the mothers weren't around, an aunt or another female made the decision. The man stayed out of it. It is not always the *macho* that rules (except, it often seems, over what beer to buy or what football game to see), it is more often the *mamacita*. Yes, in our culture, the woman has power and she wields it with extraordinary skill.

When it comes to buying automobile insurance, the dynamic is slightly more subtle. "You do the research, honey," the *macho* says to his wife. "Call around and find the cheapest insurance available. Give me the result, I'll make the decision."

The "dutiful" wife makes the calls, but often chooses the company not solely on the basis of price but because of other intangibles, like the reception she gets from their people: their manner of dealing with her, openness, etc. She then reports back to her husband that she's found the best company. He, pleased, makes the decision to go with the company she recommends. In fact, so sure is she of his forthcoming approval that three times out of four she's already signed a contract before even turning to her husband.

The game is to pretend that the husband makes the choice. Information is given to him, and he signs off on it. But in fact the decision is a *fait accompli* before it reaches him. Oftentimes he is merely being made to feel good; it suits his sense of worth, his *machismo.*

Author Ray Gonzalez says, "Latino *machismo* comes from five hundred years of total suppression by a dominant culture that spoke of honor but which extended no honor to the colonized people. They were caught between survival reality and powerlessness. Further constricted by the dictates of the church, the Latino male became a seething cauldron of unexpressed, justifiable anger."

Is *machismo,* then, just so much hot air, nothing more than a false front, a defense? That explanation is probably too easy (after all, the Latino *believes* in his *machismo*), but there is surely something to it. For the Latino, *machismo* is a way, even if only an unconscious and self-deluding way, of expressing independence in a world that makes him extremely dependent on everyone else.

Machismo's counterpart, *marianismo,* "the essence of womanhood in the Latino (Catholic) world," as author Esther Herrera puts it, is also ingrained into the Latino (and Latina) psyche. Herrera says that the word comes from the almost fanatic worship of the Virgin Mary that flourished in the Middle Ages when men and women, faced with the horrors of war and pestilence, needed a mother figure to mediate between the misery of man and the wrath of God. Strong, selfless, devoted to God and her family, she was—as she is today—the truly strong force in Latino life. A man might fight and supply the muscle in the fields or in urban laboring jobs, but it was the woman who did the really hard work of consolation and consolidation when external events threatened to tear the family apart.

The modern *mariana*, though, must do a different kind of mediating. In *The Maria Paradox*, Rosa Maria Gil and Carmen Inoa Vazquez describe the contemporary Latina as caught between the old-world values of womanhood (selflessness, sacrifice, "the family comes first and I don't really matter") and the exigencies of the modern world. In the Latino culture, women are supposed to be *buenas mujeres*—outwardly dependent, submissive and subservient to their men, while actually controlling their husbands' and children's lives, in effect making their decisions for them in secret. Their men put them under tremendous pressure to perpetuate this role, and as more and more Latinas enter the American workplace, they are caught in a bicultural dilemma. Finding themselves placed between two opposing currents—*entre dos aguas*—they must be both *marianas* and working women, Latino and American, aggressive executives and submissive family members at the same time.

My fifteen years of research have shown that both Latinos and Latinas find themselves in the same confusing situation. For Latinas, however, the confusion is worse since they are depended upon so much more to be the bulwark of the Latino family. One would think that the conflict would render Latinas ineffectual businesswomen, but that is not so. In fact, they are stronger than even the most ardent Latino would suppose. Women are increasingly succeeding in all kinds of businesses. Many have reached top management levels in small and large corporations. They are beginning to form a major (and quickly growing) nucleus in the echelons of middle management. Others have started small businesses which are prospering at an even faster rate than those begun by their male colleagues.

It is no paradox that Latinas tend to rise faster in Anglo and cross-cultural businesses than in strictly Latino firms. But they are rising *everywhere*, as indeed are their Anglo sisters (who share some of the same problems); in my opinion, women's coming into the workforce ranks with globalization as the most important business trend in the past decade. And Latinas are a major part of that trend.

࿔

Let's look at some striking facts:

- In 1985 the top thirty-three Latina-owned firms, generated an annual income of some $220 million. Today, the top fifty such firms generate an annual income of over one billion.
- In the past thirty years, the U.S. economy has grown by fifty-six million new jobs. Two thirds of these (64 percent) have gone to women.
- In 1996, women received 55 percent of all bachelor's degrees and 51 percent of all master's degrees.
- Women-owned small businesses are outpacing men-owned businesses by two to one.
- In a survey of 2,200 consumers by Video Storyboard Tests, it was found that eight of the ten most believable spokespersons for products are women (Candice Bergen, Elizabeth Taylor, Cybill Shepherd, Whitney Houston). A decade earlier, eight of the ten most believed spokespersons were men.

What's more, according to Alex Counts in the book *Give Us Credit,* "women borrowers prove to be more disciplined and resourceful. Their payments come in more regularly and the profits they earn benefit the entire family. (Men spend profits on themselves.)"

With as many women as men earning their graduate and post-graduate degrees, women are getting a "man's education," and in so doing are more than competing with men; they're inching ahead in the race for jobs and profits. This is not really a surprise. It was Socrates who said, "Once made equal to man, woman becomes his superior."

࿔

One "superior" Hispanic woman is Teresa McBride, president of McBride and Associates, a company specializing in integrating computer systems for Fortune 500 companies.

Her father, a former restaurant owner, taught her the basics—

not of computers, but of business in general. "Be focused," he told her. "Set high goals. Do business with honesty, integrity, and dedication. And above all, work harder than your competitors. Work smarter, too. Take advantage of every opportunity you can. Follow up. Follow up. Follow up."

At the beginning, to her, being a woman from a minority group was an asset. "It's great," she told herself. "I'll have better access to SBA loans. I'll certify my company as minority-owned, and I'll go one step further. I'll get an 8A certification, which means I can get government 'set-aside' contracts with little or no competition, and that'll give me a start."

Teresa's focused approach and strong follow-up allowed her to get an 8A certification in only three months, rather than the usual eighteen. Yet she quickly learned not to lean on "minority-disadvantaged" 8A contracts as a crutch. She focused on providing the *top service available*, and soon she was approaching large corporations that had nothing to do with government entitlements. She wanted to be chosen simply because she was *better* than her competition, not because she was a "minority." Her philosophy was simple: "*First* be the best. *Then,* if minority status can help you, throw it in as added value, but never *rely* on the minority tag."

Amazingly, she found that most corporations cared little about her minority status. They cared only about the quality of her work. "In the end, quality is all that matters," she says. "The government may think they are doing us a favor with their 'set-aside' programs, but many times they're actually restricting us because we never learn to compete."

Teresa used the 8A status to *learn* about government contracts and contracts in general, but she relied on her instincts and commitment to good planning to build a company that in ten years from the day she opened her door was billing almost $200 million a year.

She doesn't make much of the advantages or disadvantages of being a woman, but she's quick to recognize that women, like anyone in business, need support—from grandparents who help out with the kids when business must be done; from a family to lend support in times of trouble; from colleagues who "see" and implement a good idea whether it comes from a man or a woman.

"Sometimes for a woman there has to be gender reversal," she says. "Sometimes the husband has to take care of the kids or the house. But *everybody* needs someone to help, and in business, it's the best and the most creative—men or women—who win."

My own field, advertising, provides a graphic demonstration of the increased presence of women—Anglos and Latinas—in the American business world. (Much of women's success in advertising was pioneered by Charlotte Beers, the first woman CEO of the multinational ad firm Ogilvy & Mather, who throughout her career and even after she retired fought for the equality of women in advertising.) Eighty percent of all advertising jobs are held by women, and in the companies being "pitched" by the advertising agencies, more and more the people responsible for choosing which agency will represent their company are women. At Dr. Pepper, only two people were responsible for getting us in the door, and both were women. At Paragon Cable, five women and no men made the decision to hire us, then presented it to the men who gave their final blessing.

At KJS, we are well aware of these ratios, and we have molded our company and our presentation team accordingly. We know that women are pleased that other women are in the highest posts at our agency (it's the old principle that people like doing business with people with whom they feel most comfortable), and I'm convinced that one of the main reasons we got the Columbia Health Care account was because our team of presenters was composed of four women and one man (me), and I was largely silent during the meetings. Columbia's decision makers were composed of two men and twelve (!) women. Columbia spends seven million dollars per year in the Hispanic market, making them the top advertiser in their category. Without Lindy Richardson, Karen Bowling, Lourdes Nieto, and Sara Peterson on the client side, and without Kathy Sosa, Sandra Garcia, Roxanna Fernandez, and Maria Garcia on ours, I'm convinced we would not have gotten the account. Woman power—Anglos and Latinas working together—has ensured that the Columbia-KJS partnership will prosper.

Neglecting woman power can be disastrous. Recently a multinational advertising agency asked me to join them in a presentation to one of the major telecommunications companies in the United States. I was to detail how we would sell their products in the Hispanic market. There were nine of us at the presentation, eight men and one woman. We gave a great presentation and could very well have been the best company for the job, but we lost it. Three of the five people determining which agency to choose were women. I later discovered that the group that beat us was composed of three women and two men. Did we get beaten by coincidence? No. I think it was because the company who hired me neglected the force of woman power.

⌒

Are women better at business than men? A recent survey by Lawrence A. Pfaff and Associates would seem to say so. The study, conducted over twenty-four months from 1994 to 1996, included 941 managers at all levels (672 males, 269 females) from 204 organizations across seventeen states.

"Female managers—as rated by their bosses, themselves, and the people who work for them—were rated significantly better than their male counterparts," Pfaff reported. "The difference extends beyond the 'softer' skills such as communication, feedback and empowerment to such areas as decisiveness, planning and setting standards."

Indeed, employees rated female managers higher than males in nineteen of twenty skill areas. Bosses rated women higher in eighteen of the twenty, and even when they rated themselves, women scored higher in fifteen areas, though far more men were polled than women.

Women can be just as aggressive and ambitious as men, the survey showed. But women are more sensitive, more accurate, and better able to "pick up vibes" in a meeting room. Perhaps, Pfaff suggests, men tend to dominate meetings, and their more volatile style enables women to sit back and listen, understanding nuances and observing reactions. In other words, women open their minds, not their mouths!

Statistics relating strictly to Latinas are equally telling. These findings come from a study sponsored jointly by the Hispanic Chamber of Commerce and Phillip Morris:

- Women who own their own businesses tend to be younger than men—the largest age group is between thirty-five and forty-four—and comprise half of *all* Hispanic business owners aged thirty-five to fifty-four.
- Eight out of ten are married.
- Although widowed women managers outnumber widowed men, 23 percent to 10 percent, nine out of ten Latinas started their own businesses from scratch, rather than inheriting them from a family source.
- Latinas have more trouble getting loans and lines of credit than men (28 percent reported continuing problems), yet more Latinas than their male counterparts consistently describe themselves as "optimistic."
- Latinas report "minor" problems getting government support, while men said the problems "persisted"—this in the face of the fact that such support comes more easily to minority men than to minority women.
- One-third of all Latinas say they have "occasional problems to no problems" balancing work and family—exactly the same percentage as Latino men!
- Fifty-two percent of Latinas view their spouses as "extremely important" to their work. Twenty-six percent of men do.
- Latinos and Latinas regard the factors contributing to their success differently. Women stress networking, assertiveness, perseverance, and self-confidence; men stress hard work, dedication, education, and knowledge and experience.
- Latinas feel they're less likely to find help through training workshops and instead emphasize social and interpersonal factors as the means for advancement.
- Latina-owned businesses have shorter track records *but are equally competitive.*

∽

While the statistics are revealing, it's the women themselves who give the strongest testimony to their own success.

Bonnie Garcia, for example, became the director of Hispanic marketing for Coca-Cola, working her way from the bottom rung on the ladder to the top. Her first job was as a disc jockey, where she learned the art of aggressive promotion and how to tie products into media. But she wanted a career in a large corporation and in her early twenties went to the Stroh Brewery Company in Detroit where she learned about national marketing and distribution. When she moved to Coke, she quickly rose from PR assistant to director of the Hispanic division where, as she puts it, she "rattled the cage," finding new solutions to old problems and making up rules as she went along. She increased Coke's market share significantly, whereas her two male predecessors had achieved only modest growth. Her budget doubled, then tripled. Her department put out more radio and television commercials than any other. Hers became the most active Hispanic marketing department in the country, and if you went to see her, you'd find her in the corner office on the "sacred" seventh floor of Coke's headquarters in Atlanta. Not bad for a woman with only a high school education!

My daughters are successful, too. Anna's an accomplished painter, Rebecca's a resourceful salesperson of arts and crafts, and Blanca handles payables and receivables for a well-established glass company. I admire them greatly because they've achieved their success mostly on their own, or at least with little help from me. They (and their brother, James) had a rough start because, as I've said, I virtually abandoned them after my divorce. I was off building a business, not realizing I could have built a business *and* remained close to them if I had made that a goal.

But from the time Cristina—my youngest daughter—was three years old, I've read to her and talked about the advantages of school, her future and her success. When she was in high school, I took her on tours of college campuses and made a "deal" with her. "You're smart enough to be admitted to any university you want," I told her. "Pick any one anywhere in the world, and I'll make sure you can make that choice."

Cristina remembered our deal. Her grades were excellent, she took summer jobs, she did volunteer work, she grew interested in sports and sculpture. Last year, as a high school senior, she chose Yale as her college and, with no further help from me—she didn't want me to write letters for her, or use the influence of any of my friends—she was accepted.

Will she go into business? I don't know. And, really, I don't care. She's on her way. I've told her story not to brag, or to point out how special Cristina is—*all* kids are special—but to emphasize that if you have a goal, if you don't lose sight of it, and if you think you deserve it, it can be yours.

Was it easy for Cristina, a Hispanic woman, to achieve her educational goal at age 18? *Yes!* Because in her mind, that goal was reachable from the start. When you believe you can—you can.

Indeed, women are making it big in all areas of American business. A recent issue of *Hispanic Business* profiled a number of women *under forty*, with incomes in six or seven figures. Among them are Julie Martinez, president of Will Rent Inc. in Chicago, a real estate firm with billing of over $2.3 million; Graciela Gonzalez, who with finacé Henry Juarez started a construction business in Houston now worth over $700,000; Debbie and Susan Marquez, who on an investment of $10,000 started a Mexican restaurant in Vail, Colorado, and grossed $1 million in 1995; Carrie Monroy de Herrera, who started a private process-serving business in Sacramento, California, and last year made $180,000; Betty Lou Gamez-Fiel who opened her own temporary and permanent placement service in San Antonio and earned $581,000 in 1995; and Livia Arnaiz, a management consultant for GEM technology in Miami with billings of $2.6 million.

These women, like the thousands of other Latinas in the workplace, share traits that bring them success:

1. Latinas have a positive mental attitude.
2. Latinas are persistent.
3. Latinas are good at communicating to women *and* to men.
4. Latinas trust people and take them into their confidence.

5. Latinas can empower other employees; they can "let go" of their subordinates, "give them wings."
6. Latinas are approachable.
7. Latinas are good team leaders and members.
8. Latinas have a sense of humor. (Lawrence Pfaff found this in his survey. Laughter releases tension, and Latina humor tends to defuse uptight men, both Hispanic and Anglo.)

⤴

The road is clearly open. Yet I don't mean to say that it's easy, that all a Latina need do to be a success in business is to enter the workplace. For purposes of this book, I've conducted interviews and focus groups with dozens of Latina businesswomen. I assumed that I would get a torrent of complaints. Instead, they loved telling me about the successes. Their attitude is so positive—much more positive than their male counterparts'—that it was difficult to get them to express anything but satisfaction.

"Tell me about your problems," I'd urge. They'd speak of *individual* problems, specific to their businesses, then spend the next hour and a half telling me how they solved them. It was obvious that they'd developed very thick skins. The problems seem to energize them, invigorate them. Several said, "There are so many problems that have come my way, I've actually become an expert at jumping over them." "The bigger the challenge the greater my energy" is the prevailing attitude. "I actually enjoy jumping over barriers, or breaking them down."

Most Latina businesswomen are successful networkers, and they use their natural instincts for nurturing to get together and exchange experiences, comforting each other and lending support.

Still, there *are* problems common to them all, problems quite different from those men face. Here are some of them:

- Eliciting genuine and wholehearted support, both emotional and practical, from their husbands
- Spending enough quality time with their husbands
- Juggling family, community, and business responsibilities

- Determining what value to place on their work (not under-charging for their product or service)
- Negotiating the best deal from their suppliers
- Fighting aggressively enough for raises for themselves (they're often terrific at fighting for their people)
- Finding time to develop their professionalism at schools and seminars
- Working on "contingency" rather than on a preset business plan ("Too often we have to put out fires.")
- Obtaining loans to grow
- Training good people
- Overcoming intimidating men
- Defending against patronizing men
- Getting taken seriously
- Combating discrimination because of Latina-ness (a problem I had thought women would put first, but which my interviewees actually placed in the last quadrant)

Women tend to list twice as many problems as men. Men's complaints cover lack of financing, finding good people, discrimination, lack of opportunity, and lack of training. When men list problems in business, they tend to feel that the causes come from forces over which they have no control. Latinas put their problems on their own backs.

No matter what face they put on them, however, the women's problems are real and it will take years to overcome them all. Remember, Latinas are relatively new in the workplace. Still, there's ample evidence that change for the better is not only possible but already with us. One support group for Latinas is a national association called BPW, or Business and Professional Women. They have a chapter in virtually every city, town, or community in the U.S. The women who join tend to prosper. They teach and learn *como ponerse los pantalones*—how to put on the pants.

In many important ways, they already have.

CHAPTER 11

WHICH OF MY FACES SHOULD I SHOW?

¿Cuál de mis caras quiero que vean?

Latinas must show one aspect at home, another in the workplace. But all Latinos, in effect, share the same problem.

My friend the comedian Paul Rodriguez tells a joke that gets a big laugh every time. He talks about being in downtown Los Angeles and getting on an elevator to visit his agent in one of the office buildings there. He looks around and finds himself surrounded by Asians, all chattering away in Chinese. "Boy, did I get pissed off," he says. "Don't those people know where they are? This is America! They should be speaking Spanish!"

The roomful of Latinos howl. Paul, of course, loves it. He just told a joke *in English* to Latinos about Spanish and Chinese. Everyone understands it because they understand how easily we can move from one culture to the other, from one language to the other.

Early on in your business career, you'll have to answer a vital question, one that goes not only to the heart of your public persona but to your inner core as well—*Which of my faces do I want them to see?*

Indeed, we have that option. As Latinos, most of us have many "faces." Some of us are mostly Latino with a touch of Americanization mixed in; others are mostly "gringo" with only traces of our Latino-ness. It is sometimes essential to move from one culture/language to the other. Some of us are true chameleons, depending on the circumstances.

There is nothing strange here. Greek, Italian, Jewish, Jamaican, and Irish immigrants have had to go through the same process; I've heard one of my African-American friends speak "black" English in bars with his pals, "white" English in business meetings. For us, the more we can assume different "faces" at will, the better we'll be able to get on in American life, both in our neighborhoods and at work.

In Texas there's a phenomenon called "Tex-Mex," a lingo used by some five million "Tejanos" and Southwest U.S. Mexican-Americans. Trinity University professor Scott Baird, quoted in an article in the San Antonio *Express News,* believes the lingo is actually becoming a distinct language. The spoken version takes English words and adds Spanish conjugations and applies English grammatical rules, but Baird says he prefers what he calls "Spanglish," a language that mixes Spanish and English words. *Parquear,* for example, means "to park" in Tex-Mex. The Spanish word is *estacionar.* Here are some more of Professor Baird's examples:

La troca	pickup truck
El lonche	lunch (*almuerzo*)
El cloche	automobile clutch
Weldear	to weld (*soldar* means to solder and to weld)
Taipear	to type (*excribir a máquina*)
Mopiar	to mop (*trapear el suelo*)
Baquear pa'atras	to back up
El mofle	muffler (*amortiguador*)
Me estás kiddiando	you're kidding me
La marqueta	market
Los tenis	tennis shoes (contraction of *los zapatos de tenis*)

Many linguists disagree that Tex-Mex is a language, but language or lingo, it demonstrates the acculturation process vividly. We Latinos draw closer and closer to our Anglo brothers and sisters. As in life, so in business.

⁎

The most frequently asked questions in regard to Hispanic marketing are: Aren't Latinos themselves very different from one another—aren't Mexicans different from Cubans who are different from Puerto Ricans and from Hondurans? And thus don't we need different advertising campaigns for the same product in Miami, say, and Texas? In New York and California?

Well, yes and no. There *are* differences among Latino groups, and sometimes a campaign can build on them. A Budweiser spot that runs in Miami might have *cumbias* as the music background, with people playing on the beach, while a Texas spot might feature Tejano music and wrangler-type Latinos around a picnic table. But since it's cheaper and frequently just as effective to produce one advertisement to be used nationally, most marketers concentrate on the similarities among the groups—*somos una raza*—not the differences.

For the similarities predominate. Imagine the United States as being made up of different countries, not states. People from Mississippi and Maine are surely as different as people from Nicaragua and Puerto Rico; a New York cabbie, a Cajun from New Orleans, a California surfer, and a Wisconsin dairy farmer have different dialects, different values, different goals, different dreams. Yet advertisers have no trouble creating campaigns that appeal to all of them in English—the same campaigns, in fact, that "play" in Greece and Germany, Sweden and Singapore. After all, network TV is one national spot, not several regional ones.

The *real* differences among American Latino groups have to do with how long they've been in the U.S., their degree of fluency in English, their neighborhoods—in other words, their degree of acculturation.

As marketers planning local campaigns, we've developed basic techniques for identifying and understanding these differences. We need to know:

- Where do the people we're trying to reach live?
- Where do they work?
- Where do they play?
- Where do they shop?
- What media do they listen to and read (Spanish, English, or both)?
- What language do they speak at home? At work? With their friends? With their kids? With their parents and grandparents?

So important is this information that we've incorporated it into maps, with the darkest areas showing where the Spanish-dominant Latinos tend to live, the medium gray areas where the bilingual, bicultural Hispanics live, and the light gray areas the most Americanized Latinos. After fifteen years of research we can depict Latino population density in Los Angeles and Miami, in Dallas and Houston and (of course) San Antonio to a high degree of accuracy.

When we know the answers, we can reach the potential buyer or user with sophistication. Our maps help us pinpoint our customers for local promotions and events. On network television, say, or in national magazines, marketers play to the Latino similarities. A solely Spanish-speaking Latino drinks as much Coke as one who speaks only English. The smart marketer doesn't reach one and leave the other out. *Lo quieren todo*—they want it all—as well they should.

What does all this have to do with *your* business? Your success in America?

Well, your level of acculturation is strongly tied to your success. Read on.

⌐

American business is speeding ahead in terms of growth and technology. *El tren se va*—the train is on its way. I've used the image of business-as-train before; now it's time to use it again, this time as it relates to acculturation:

The illustration concentrates on your degree of fluency in English, for without mastery, your prospects for optimum success are dimmed if not eradicated. Of course, if you start a business in a strictly Spanish-speaking neighborhood and do not wish to move beyond it, English is not essential (though even in this case it would help; it always does). I know several Spanish-language-only millionaires in Miami. For the rest of you, you'll need it as the essential ticket to board the train.

And mastery of English means having a good vocabulary but also knowing the American idiom and how to use it. You need to know sports and other "guy" things (sports *are* an important venue for business communication). You must know "gal" things too—fashion, makeup, relationships. You can't excel in business without understanding nuance. Once, at a meeting in Ecuador, talking with a CEO who knew fluent "book English," I described our negotiation as "a done deal." "Don deel, what is that?" the CEO asked. "A new card game in Las Vegas?" (He knew about Vegas, but I did have to explain.) Imagine not knowing that idiom in the U.S., I thought. The guy might make a sale and not know it. The deepest friendships depend largely on language; business ease depends, to an even greater extent, on language. If you miss nuance, you may well bypass opportunity. And if you worry about what someone *might* mean, you're very likely to miss what he or she says next, and maybe miss the thrust of an entire negotiation.

As we all know, it is a tremendous business advantage to be fluent in English. After all, it is the language of business around the world. In the Brazilian business community, English is spoken almost as often as Portuguese, and much more than Spanish, even though Brazil is in Latin America. If you're reading this book in English, you're probably English-dominant or English-preferred. You're on your way—*estás listo.* If you're reading it in Spanish, find a good English teacher and study hard!

Latinos who speak only English, however, are also at a distinct disadvantage. Third- and fourth-generation Latinos may find it difficult to go back to the language of their ancestors. Yet they (and maybe you) should make every effort to do so. Knowing your culture and your roots is good. But you must also be in direct touch with the prime component of your heritage, the Spanish language. It is an unparalleled business tool. If it's rusty, I urge you to relearn your language. If you can afford to travel, Cuernavaca, Mexico, boasts some twenty schools devoted expressly to reimmersion courses; if you must stay at home, take "total immersion" courses. Speak Spanish with relatives, especially parents and grandparents, and with friends as often as you can. True fluency comes only with continued use, no matter how good your teacher.

The most successful Latino businesspeople are fully *bi*lingual. And here, Latinos are at a tremendous advantage. Even if you come from a Spanish-speaking household, or if you're a third- or fourth-generation American accustomed only to English, you'll at least have an "ear" in the other language and learning it should not be difficult.

To have your feet planted firmly and equally in two cultures virtually guarantees business success. If you can work as easily with Anglos as you can with other Latinos, you can work anywhere in the hemisphere. You will become an asset to any multinational corporation; you will find yourself traveling, learning, and growing with a job security few one-language colleagues can attain.

〜

As I've worked with hugely successful Latinos over the years, I've studied their degree of acculturation. My findings aren't meant to criticize (all of them are at the top of their professions) and I don't think an entertainer, say, who is bilingual is "better" than one who speaks only one language. Still, I've had fun making up the list that follows on the next page, and I trust you'll enjoy analyzing it.

Latino Persona	Cross-Cultural Persona	Anglo Persona
Relates most easily to Latinos and Latino audiences. Feels most comfortable in Latino situations and Spanish language.	Can relate to both Latinos and Anglos with equal ease. Promotes Latino-ness while courting Anglo audiences. Is bilingual.	Relates to Anglos and Anglo audiences with ease. Feels little need to promote Latino-ness. Feels most comfortable in the English language.
Luis Miguel	Gloria Estefan	Charlie Sheen
Enrique Iglesias	Edward James Olmos	Mariah Carey
Cristina	Ricardo Montalban	Andy Garcia
Selena	Jimmy Smits	Frederico Peña
Péle	Vikki Carr	Linda Ronstadt
	Oscar de la Renta	Rosie Perez
	Henry Cisneros	Diasy Fuentes
	Desi Arnaz	Emilio Estevez
	Julio Iglesias	Lee Trevino
	Antonio Banderas	Nancy Lopez
	Elizabeth Peña	Martin Sheen
	Jennifer Lopez	Geraldo Rivera
	Jose Canseco	
	Chi Chi Rodriguez	
	Roberto Goizueta	
	Oscar de la Hoya	
	Carolina Herrera	

UNACCULTURATED   FULLY ACCULTURATED

There are some observations to be added:

- The singers Luis Miguel and Enrique Iglesias (Julio's son) have huge Latino followings, but as in the development of any international star, they are also working hard to reach an Anglo audience, just as Selena (who in her speech was English-dominant) was trying to do at the time of her death.
- Cristina, "the Latina Oprah Winfrey," who has the most successful talk show on Spanish television, has experimented with the same kind of show on English television, but it didn't fly. I think she's wonderful. But I suspect it's because she really is a bit more comfortable in Spanish.
- Péle, the soccer icon from Brazil, doesn't have to speak *any* language. He remains one of the most popular personalities in the world.

- Martin Sheen and his two sons, Charlie and Emilio, are not major successes in Latin America even though Emilio has kept his birth surname, Estevez.
- Linda Ronstadt speaks little Spanish—but sings it divinely!
- Frederico Peña is English-dominant while Henry Cisneros is fluent in both languages, telling us only that there is more than one road to a high government position.
- Lee Trevino and Nancy Lopez don't speak Spanish at all, but then again, I can't play much golf.
- Carolina Herrera has been a success in the Anglo as well as the Latino world—using international designs.

What does all this prove? Nothing more than that if you have a superabundance of talent, you will succeed, no matter what language you speak. For the rest of us, though, I recommend bilingualism and biculturation. For we are no different from any ethnic European immigrants (although we came here first); we bring our culture with us, and the better we can integrate it into American society, the richer we *and* the United States will be.

In his book *Trends 2000*, Gerald Celente predicts that one of the biggest trends to look for is what he calls "Latino chic":

> The spectacle of Vice President Al Gore doing his version of the macarena on national television is only the beginning. Trend-watchers predict a mounting wave of American enthusiasm for south-of-the-border cultures in all their rich diversity.
>
> Several developments fuel the pattern. They include: continuing population growth among Hispanic Americans, whose numbers are expected to jump from 30 million to 42 million by 2010; Hispanic buying power, which rose to $228 billion in 1996 from $94 in 1984, will climb further still; and the expected normalization of U.S. relations with Cuba, which will reinvigorate America's traditional romance with its biggest Caribbean neighbor.

Dolores Flores, of southwest Detroit, puts it this way:

> There are a lot of Latinos who have done wonders for our community. Selena helped make the music popular, and I

think it will get bigger. But I also think we need to get together in the Latino community to help our own people. I am tremendously proud of my heritage and rejoice when I see signs of it in the American landscape (my home is in San Antonio, not "Saint Anthony"). Yes, we are all immigrants. So is practically everyone else in this country save Native Americans. I am Latino *and* American. And proud of it.

It's clear that the bicultural Latino actually has an *advantage* in the Anglo business world. But he or she must still know the rudiments of business. And he or she must know how to negotiate.

CHAPTER 12

DOING THE DEAL

Haciendo buen negocio

Three years after the opening of my art design studio—the one I had promised myself would be the best in all Texas—much of our business consisted of designing corporate logos. In fact, we were responsible for two-thirds of all the logos in our marketing area. Gas stations, fast-food chains, banks, oil companies, soft-drink manufacturers, automobile dealerships: it was impossible to drive anywhere in south Texas without seeing something designed by Sosart.

The trouble was that designing logos, while a wonderful way to promote our agency because of their visibility, didn't lead to recurring income. Once designed, the logo wouldn't change, and I'd have to find another logo to design. Advertising agencies depend on *continuing* income. We needed a corporation's campaign year after year. But we were based in San Antonio, where nothing much was happening. Houston was booming and Dallas was home to major corporations; it was in those cities that our main competition lay. Why would a major firm give their business to an agency, no matter how good, in remote San Antonio?

It was a situation that seemed to mean my goal would remain unfulfilled, at least for a while.

One day, when my secretary was out, a man came to see me without an appointment. He was dressed casually; his shoes were designed for comfort, not style. He was in his early forties, neat but hardly prepossessing, yet there was a twinkle in his eye and a straightforwardness to his manner that made me like him immediately.

"My name's Dave Bamberger. I'm with Church's Fried Chicken," he told me. "We need help with our image, and with our employee incentive programs. I've seen your graphics—goodness, they're all over the state!—and I thought maybe you'd be able to help us. We'd like you to design something that'll do two things at once: motivate our people to stay with the company, and increase sales of our fried chicken to the public. Interested?"

"Of course," I said, though I figured this was another smallish project. After all, this man was obviously from middle management at best, sent to scout out a few vendors. Nevertheless, it didn't hurt to talk, and talk we did—for two hours that day, and for an even longer period at a second meeting, then a third.

Each time, Dave came to my office. Each time, the informality of our conversation mirrored the informality of his clothes. I began to look on him more as a friend than as a client, and together we began to develop what came to be known as the Master Merchant Program, aimed at motivating Church's employees and increasing sales. Dave wanted his crew members to happily cook and serve his delicious fried chicken.

We designed snappy uniforms and merit badges. We produced videos and slide shows as well as booklets to train the personnel on how to do each aspect of their jobs better. Then we devised ways by which they could earn merit badges. There was a badge for becoming a Master Cook, another for becoming a Master Team Member, still another for becoming a Master Merchant when the store sales increased by more than ten percent over the same quarter a year before.

We designed promotions around "prominent chickens in

history"—we gave them names like Eddie Rickenchicken (a World War II bird) to Chicken Little to the famous acting chicken Gregory Peck. Our team worked like hell and we loved it. Dave became our buddy, one of us. Our "presentations" to him were informal and familial—a give and take of ideas—of creativity.

After many meetings he turned to me with a smile. "Guys and gals, let's make our association official. You're our ad agency," he said. "You're on for a monthly retainer of fifty thousand dollars. Fair?"

Fair? It was *¡fabuloso!* And exactly the kind of long-term business our agency was looking for, the kind of client that would put us on the map. I was amazed that a middle manager had the authority to make such a deal, but I, of course, said nothing about it and gladly accepted.

"Draw up the contract," he said. "Then, when you're ready, come down to the office and we'll sign it."

Three days later I was at Church's Fried Chicken headquarters for the first time, contract in hand. I was ushered into Dave's office immediately. It was a corner office, wonderfully spacious and beautifully decorated. Behind a huge desk sat Dave, grinning. Middle management? He was executive vice president and chief operating officer, the man who along with Bill Church grew Church's Fried Chicken from three outlets to over a thousand in less than ten years. All that time, I had been dealing with the most important man in the company except for Bill Church himself!

Almost unwittingly I had made an excellent deal for the agency. If I had known Dave really was the chief honcho, would the deal have been so easily consummated? After all, he was the COO of a multi-million-dollar company, I a small graphics designer. If, instead of showing up unannounced at my office, Dave had had his secretary summon me to his grand office, would I have felt free to express myself so frankly? Would I have been so confident, so at ease, so much his equal?

The answer is easy: No way. I would have probably called him "Mr. Bamberger" from the beginning. We would have had an aloof "business relationship" and never become buddies. What made the difference was that I thought he was a regular guy. He fooled me into being my best. We kept Church's business for years—until Dave retired with forty million dollars (1976 dollars) in his pocket. We went to each other's homes, got to know each other's wives and kids. We exchanged success stories and failure stories and I introduced him to several friends, some of whom he went into business with after "retirement."

＊

There are two important deal-making lessons in the Church's story. First, you cannot make the best deal unless you have confidence. Second, confidence comes from feeling equal. I knew our agency was good, and I had my dream always in mind—both essential factors in any negotiation. But not enough. To your own skill and your own goal you have to add a sense of ease. If you're intimidated, if you think the person you're dealing with is your "superior," then you're at a tremendous disadvantage. Experienced negotiators will pick up on your insecurity; most will use it to sweeten their side of the bargain.

Granted, the people on the other side of the table may indeed be your "superiors," if only in terms of income and title. But most of the time, they need you as much as or more than you need them. And as you succeed, you'll find that you earn more than your customers or clients.

Oprah Winfrey has an excellent solution. "When I started out as a reporter," she says, "I didn't see myself as a young black woman asking questions of important people. Instead, I stepped into a character—into Barbara Walters. And *nobody* turns Barbara Walters away!"

She pretended to be somebody else, and her insecurity vanished. Another possibility is to pretend that the person you're dealing with is someone else; in the last chapter, we saw how effective that method can be. I didn't have to pretend Dave Bamberger was someone else—I *believed* he was, from the start. Eyeball to eyeball, I was his equal, his friend. Together we were working toward the solution best for both of us. But in the real world most of the time you know the position of the person facing you. Don't let it intimidate you. Use this "pretend" technique.

Anton Chekhov said, "A man is what he believes." According to W. Somerset Maugham, "If you refuse to accept anything but the best, very often you get it." And Jesse Jackson advises, simply, "Keep your eye on the prize." There is even a Spanish *dicho: "El que no habla, Dios no lo oye"*—he who doesn't ask, doesn't get.

All these dicta are the foundations of good negotiating. Oprah Winfrey exemplifies Chekhov's, which naturally applies to women as well as men. In my dealing with Dave Bamberger, I felt free to follow the philosophies of Maugham and Jackson because I *believed* Dave and I were equals.

Confidence. A sense of equality. The more you feel them, the more you have them. And the better the deals you will make.

Still, it's tough to feel equal to a CEO, marketing director, or potential client if you are one of a number of applicants and you really need the business to survive. Every book on negotiations tells you that you have to be prepared to "walk away" from a deal if it doesn't suit you, and they're right, but it's not so easy if the deal is super-important and there are no other prospective clients in sight.

The problem is that the more needy you are, the more inferior you feel—and the less likely you are to make or negotiate the best deal. What usually happens is that you freeze. Your spontaneous, creative mind is overruled by a voice that says, "Watch out! Don't screw up! Am I doing okay? What'll the client think if our proposal is off base? If I ask for too much? If I don't really understand what my client wants? If I piss him off? If I seem like a bozo?"

Imagine yourself at a social evening with just the president and the first lady and no one else for four hours, and you'll see what I mean. In that situation, we'd either show off, clam up, or just die. We'd forget that even the president and his wife are just people. Whatever qualities we have would be submerged in awkwardness and artificiality.

Such a situation would be particularly difficult for most Latinos, so it's not surprising that when we're thrust alone into confrontations with the "powerful," our ease disappears. My mom would say *"es un americano,"* meaning "he's an Anglo." But by saying "he's an American," she was unwittingly implying we were not. Many of us still use this phrase. Oh, the power of subtle wording!

Where Anglos are brought up to be independent, our culture teaches us to be *inter*dependent, and it holds us back in business situations. As babies, we're wrapped in blankets and carried at our mother's breast—indeed the mother will sacrifice the use of her hands for other jobs to make sure we're secure and protected. Sheltering is a requisite of love in our culture, whereas the Anglo mother will carry her baby on her back, or jog along the road pushing her baby in a stroller in front of her.

No wonder, then, that our heart begins to pound when we're one-on-one with a client we perceive as "powerful" or somehow more "American" (meaning more deserving) than us. No sheltering is possible. Instinctively, we seek protection. But in business we must learn to rely on ourselves first. On our confidence. On our equality.

Here are the six steps you must master before you can deal in business successfully.

1. Establish confidence by believing in yourself as the equal to anyone.

Take this test: Next time you're at a business meeting with Anglos, at a cocktail party with your clients or "superiors," at a Chamber of Commerce meeting, or simply in a one-on-one conversation with a stranger where you're not sure of your intellectual ground, tune out for a moment on what's being said and tune in to your inner self.

You may find that you feel a desire to flee— *"Me tengo que salir."* You may feel queasy and want to go home, or you may find yourself casting your eyes around the room hoping to find a friendly face or a place where you can stand unobtrusively out of the limelight.

Let's say you're at a party talking to an Anglo. You may or may not be doing business with him in the future, but right now that's not the point. You're having a social conversation, and you feel at ease. The Anglo is friendly, welcoming, interested in your views. The Anglo begins to talk about a subject unfamiliar to you, maybe something as mundane as a skiing trip. You've never been on skis in your life. You try to turn the conversation back to the familiar ground you were on before, but a third person joins you and enthusiastically begins discussing the relative merits of Sun Valley versus Vail.

At this point, listen not to them but to your feelings. An inner voice is probably saying, "Run! You don't belong here. Get out before you make a fool of yourself." It's telling you to look at your watch and say, "My goodness. I didn't realize how late it was getting. I really should be going home."

The moral here is that if you can articulate to yourself your feelings of discomfort, you can live through them. All of us experience awkwardness, but if we can become *familiar* with the sensation, if it's something we've faced directly before, then more and more we can master the art of getting past it.

Again, you might pretend the person you're speaking to is a high school buddy. "Wow! I've never been skiing. What's it like?" Or you can switch the talk from an unfamiliar sport like skiing to baseball, football, soccer, or whatever your favorite may me. Make a joke about it.

The moment you're able to joke with strangers or feel secure about something you know nothing about is the moment you won't want to run. When people know something you don't, they want to tell you all about it. Let them. They'll enjoy it and you'll learn something to use later.

And in a negotiation, when the bargaining gets tough or a point comes up that you have not anticipated, if you can recognize your own desire to "run"—to give in to the demand or concede the point simply because you want the negotiation to end—you'll be able to stand firm or at least say, "I haven't thought about that. Please go through it again so I can be sure I understand what you're saying."

Giving in on a deal because you're uncomfortable can be disastrous. On the other hand, conceding a point because you see it's a win-win situation is good business. There's quite a difference! It's the essence of good negotiation.

2. Define your goal. Know what you want and what you're willing to sacrifice to make the deal.

Some people go into meetings hoping something good will come of them—*ojalá que salga todo bien*—without clearly knowing what they want beyond a "favorable deal." Such people generally come out with little or nothing.

It's essential to visualize the end result before any negotiation starts, and it's essential to visualize the connecting steps from start to finish. It's not enough for me to think "I want the account." I must have a deep desire to win it. I have to know how much income it will bring in, how much work we'll have to do to get it, and the minimum fee I'll be willing to take to win the client.

Before starting any negotiation, take the time to decide what you want the result to be. My advice here is to think big. When I approached Coca-Cola, I wanted the whole account, not a piece of it. Once, when Al Aguilar negotiated with Burger King, he asked for a $750,000 net fee, not the $300,000 they proposed, and he proved how much better a job he could do *for them* with the larger sum. In those two cases we thought big and everybody won, the clients and us. Of course, at times you'll have to come down from the top of the mountain to a place somewhere *near* the top. That's okay. Just make sure the mountain is really high.

If you ask for a dollar, you'll probably wind up with seventy-five cents. If you ask for *two* dollars, you might settle at $1.25. I always ask for more than I think I'm going to get, *but I always know the bottom-line figure I won't go under.*

It's vital to have the ability to walk away from a deal. This is where self-confidence ultimately comes in. Time and again I've seen entrepreneurs sell themselves short, thinking, "If I take a loss now, I'll make up the business in the renegotiation. *Algo es mejor que nada*—something's better than nothing." But if you accept a smaller-than-profitable sum to begin with, that's the figure that the renegotiation starts with.

Al's deal with Burger King turned out wonderfully for both parties. The relationship between agency and company has lasted ten years with an approximate ten-percent raise for the agency every year. Imagine if Al had agreed to the initial fee of $300,000 rather than holding out for $750,000. It would have meant $30,000 more a year rather than $75,000. You do the math.

Huge corporations can take losses on individual facets of their business as part of research and development or as a means of enlarging the corporation as a whole. But small businesses without capital reserves and with limited borrowing power should always negotiate some profit to start with—and always make sure there's a clause that allows them to renegotiate in six to twelve months.

Sometimes you may be able to justify taking a small loss to land a client, just because acquisition of the client is so prestigious you'll be able to attract other profitable business because of it. But beware! You must win along with your client. Know the least you can accept and stick to it.

3. Put yourself in their shoes.

The more you do business, the more you'll be able to see the other's point of view—and the better your ability to negotiate will be. If you can accurately anticipate the needs and wishes of the other, then you'll be able to formulate a deal that will satisfy you both.

At the office, we play a game before we go into any negotiation. One of us pretends that he or she is the person we're bringing the deal to and negotiates with us just as hard as the prospective client is likely to. We'll have done a lot of research before the game begins, so the negotiator from "their side" will know real figures, real schedules, and just how much is likely to be demanded in terms of our effort and resources.

Define the client's culture and the nature of their business before you start out. In our case, a creative campaign for Coke, say, won't work for Joy dishwashing liquid. Joy will require different strategies, different schedules, different resources, different strengths. A is *always* different from B. Every deal has unique characteristics, every client has different needs, every negotiation brings different results. The more you can empathize with your client before and during the negotiation, the easier the negotiation will be. And remember: The idea is not to have a winner and loser. The idea is to make sure both parties win.

Years ago, in the infancy of my agency, I had a partner with whom I could not get along. Skillful and talented though she was, our personality differences were too great, and we decided to go our separate ways. Her partnership shares in the company amounted to twenty percent, mine eighty percent. I volunteered to buy her out.

"I want two hundred thousand dollars," she announced.

The company was not worth anywhere near a million dollars.

"What you're asking would represent more than a twenty-percent share. But let me make you a counteroffer. *You* buy *me* out for eight hundred thousand dollars. If you think the company is worth a million, surely that would be fair."

We agreed on a lower sum. Today, as friends, we laugh about the negotiation. "I learned something," she says. "You gotta see both sides."

4. Think as a businessperson, not as a "minority" businessperson.

For purposes of this book, I organized a focus group of Anglo and Latino businesspersons, purchasing leaders, and personnel officers to discuss the common mistakes we Latinos make when we deal with Anglo businesses. I myself was aware that Latinos are far more orally oriented than Anglos, that our word is all we need to complete a deal. Anglos, however, want the deal in writing. I'm not saying we trust each other more (it's a matter of style), but surely Anglos insist on precise definition—scope, delivery dates, budgets, etc.—with nothing left to memory or chance. When dealing with them we must confirm verbal deals in writing. It doesn't have to be complicated, just clear and concise. I've seen the simplest transactions covered in documents of ten pages or more, and sometimes that's too much "stuff." Don't get caught up in paperwork.

In any event, here's what the focus group brought out:

- Latinos ask fewer questions. That's when we don't think out all the details far enough ahead. The result is that Anglos assume we *do* understand and are surprised when disputes arise later.
- Latinos take fewer notes. We think we can remember—and sometimes we don't (or remember imprecisely). I can always spot a good advertising person, whether in account service or creative. In client meetings, he or she *takes notes at precisely the right times.* When something important is said—note.

When there's conversation with little substance—no notes. It's an art to separate the wheat from the chaff, but when putting business deals in writing, even at a preliminary stage, you must do it.

- We don't always exchange business cards, and we aren't always aware of titles. Sometimes we think that a conversation with an administrative assistant is tantamount to a deal. This can lead us to express the right idea to the wrong person.

- We may not always research the company we're dealing with. We take what we're told about it at face value when we should be fully familiar with the product and the organizational chart. (I'm painfully aware of this one. Years ago, we were negotiating with McCann Erickson, Coke's worldwide advertising agency, to be the Hispanic subagent for Coca-Cola. At the very first meeting, when we were offered something to drink, one of my team members asked for a Dr Pepper! It took us three years before we could again negotiate for the account.)

- Sometimes, we badmouth our competition. Your product or service should speak for itself, and competition should be implicit rather than explicit. If, on the other hand, you acknowledge and even praise the competition when appropriate, it shows class, character, and confidence. A client once told me we got the account because our competition told him we were not as creative as our reputation implied, and besides that, I wouldn't be personally involved. He didn't believe it.

- We sometimes exchange "poor me" stories of previous disasters, thinking they're amusing or attractively self-deprecating. Folks will tend to believe that a previous failure will be repeated.

- We aren't well enough prepared with charts and other visuals. *"Es mucho borlete,"* we tell ourselves—it's too much bother. Anglos are accustomed to top-notch presentations. They feel that's the best way of getting your message across, and they expect them at any presentation. They're not expensive; you can prepare them on a laptop. It behooves you to learn to use presentation software like PowerPoint.

- Latinos are overly grateful when granted an opportunity or meeting. We sometimes overdo our "wow." When we do, others assume that we haven't been at many meetings or been granted that many other opportunities before. They may even look on us with suspicion. Learn to take meetings and opportunities with great class, even somewhat matter-of-factly.

5. Be prepared to discuss details.

I've said that the big picture is critical, and it is. You must have your goal clearly in mind, know what the deal is supposed to accomplish, have the whole project fully formed before you even start the negotiation. But if you neglect the details, all your strategic thinking will be worth nothing.

I learned the hard way. A few years ago, I decided I would publish a guidebook to San Antonio. A colleague wrote it; my designers illustrated it. All I needed was a printer. I would be the distributor. No such book existed; mine, I figured, would sell year after year and become the standard guide for all San Antonio's visitors.

If we ordered 100,000 copies, each book could be printed for about a dollar. We would sell the guides at $3.95. Even with the discount to booksellers, I would still make a substantial profit.

It was a splendid idea, I thought, and it fulfilled many of the criteria I had set up about new ventures: It filled a definite need; it could be produced at reasonable cost; I had control over the final product. Since I had thought it through and come up with the "big picture," it was a "go."

But I had forgotten one detail. There was no way I was ever going to sell 100,000 copies!

If I had done my homework, I would have discovered that no book printed about San Antonio had ever sold more than 25,000 copies. Most had sold ten to fifteen thousand. In my desire to reduce the cost, I had printed many more books than I could sell. Amazingly, I sold 35,000. But I wound up with 65,000 books that rotted in a warehouse—and a debt of $70,000 that took me years to repay.

There is a simple lesson here: When you think big, you must also think through.

6. Recognize the best offer, and be flexible enough to adjust to it.

Money is not the only measure of the worth of an offer. Future business, networking, relationships, prestige—all these can have a bearing on the deal you're making. *"Hay que considerar todo"*— you've got to consider everything. There are some products, for instance, I wouldn't market no matter how much I was offered, and there are campaigns I'd take on for cost only.

Fifteen years ago we wanted to hire a new marketing director. After a protracted search, we found an ideal candidate. Since we were still a small company, I offered him a good but hardly extraordinary starting salary and promised him a percentage of profits throughout his tenure at the agency. He turned us down in favor of a far higher salary at a different agency. But there he got no percentage, and to this day he regrets his decision. We grew as I had predicted we would. But he opted for immediate gain without thinking of the long-term possibilities.

⌒

Like everybody else, we've made good deals and bad ones. Much of negotiation is instinct, and that comes with experience. Be careful, do your homework, follow the rules I've set down. At worst you won't be badly hurt, at best you'll prosper.

But no matter how good the deal, it will gain you little if you don't run your own business like a business—the subject of the next chapter.

CHAPTER 13

RUN YOUR BUSINESS LIKE A BUSINESS

No es un juego

This chapter and the next concern fundamental business principles, no different for Latinos than they are for Anglos. As many Anglos as Latinos start up their businesses without business plans, financial projections, marketing strategies, even clearly defined goals (beyond making "lots of money"). They can't find investors for such ventures, since there is not enough solid information to judge by. But somehow it hurts me more when a Latino starts a business without a carefully thought-through plan than when an Anglo does. The average Latino may fail no matter whom he turns to, whereas the Anglo *might* find an investor, thanks to the fact that more people will listen to his plan.

The Latino starting out in a new business is likely to be less trusted by those with money to put into that business—banks, other businesses, individuals—and while this is unfair, it is the reality.

So it is even more important for Latinos to run their businesses based on a sound, well-developed plan. We must acknowledge that we start at a disadvantage, and at the very least we must anticipate every question and envision how we will overcome every obstacle before we look for investors, or if we have adequate start-up capital, before we set up shop.

⌇

When Latinos face serious problems, business or personal, often-times we solve them in one of two ways: We rely on God, or we rely on luck.

Remember the "business plan" I described in chapter 1?

Lo que Dios quiera—whatever God wants.
Como Dios quiera—however God wants it.
Así lo quiere Dios—that's the way God wanted it.

This fatalistic approach is what our conquerors taught us and, in many of our Latino neighborhoods, is what our church teaches us today. By relying on God, we will be virtuous, "correct." In this world, we are taught, we won't wind up with much in the way of material goods, but we will have lived the good life and we will achieve our ultimate goal: we will go to heaven.

When Latinos are sick, we prefer traditional home remedies to make us well. We hate to go to the doctor except when it *really* hurts.

The same is true in business. We tend to rely on luck more than we should. In the old country, we would trust in magic, even believing that good luck can be furthered through the use of magic powders, *polvitos*. These *polvitos*, which some Latinos still use (although more in Latin America than in the United States), are the magic needed to solve almost any problem. Here are four *polvitos* featured in a 1997 desk calendar called *Hecho en México*:

1. *El legítimo polvo contra la envidia*—the authentic powder to combat envy. Used just before anyone visits. "This will keep me from harm and prevent the visitor from feeling envy or spreading malicious gossip."

2. *El legítimo polvo contra el olvido*—the legitimate powder to combat forgetfulness. "If I powder myself with this after my bath, my memory will become strong."

3. Rattlesnake sperm (how about *that?*), used in voodoo or *santería*, which when ingested will chase away the devil and guarantee success in any venture.
4. *Jabón para todo*—the soap for everything. Perhaps most potent of all. "This will improve my powers of domination, bring me good luck, make sure divine providence shines on me and brings me wealth and peace."

I suppose by taking them all, I might lead a worry-free, always successful life. But I prefer to rely on something I believe in more strongly: myself.

⌒

Actually, I believe in the power of believing, not in the efficacy of rattlesnake sperm (except for other rattlesnakes). To succeed in business, don't *depend* on God (although He'll always be there to help), and don't depend on luck. *Do* depend on a goal, a good business plan, and your own powers, your own abilities.

If you're like most Latinos, you already possess many "success" traits, whether you know it or not. In business, these are the ones that come naturally:

- Your friendliness, as demonstrated in the *abrazo* and in your caring for others
- Your desire to please and to be of service
- Your desire to work hard, as exemplified in the phrase *"No quiero que me den, quiero que me pongan donde hay"*—I don't want anything given to me, I just want to be where there's something to get
- Your desire to learn and your assumption that others have the same desire
- Your capacity for taking risks (after all, how else did you or your parents get to America?)
- Your street smarts, the ability to survive on your own
- Your capacity to dream, to imagine the best (The very fact that you're reading this book proves it.)

But watch out! You also have traits you should consciously shun:

- Your inclination to settle for modest goals
- Your tendency to include family in whatever you do
- Your hesitancy to relocate
- A belief that you *should* grab all you can before anyone else does, a philosophy prevalent in Mexico and other parts of Latin America where everyone is out to get everybody before someone gets him. (In the United States we also have wheeling and dealing, politics and business as usual, but here we've developed legal ways to make it "ethical"—a Mexican judge is "on the take," while an American judge can accept political contributions from lawyers he'll see in the courtroom. In Mexico politicians are "bought," whereas American interests hire lobbyists and consultants to convince politicians to see things their way—yet, that said, Latinos in general have fewer scruples than gringos.)
- Your capacity for accepting things as they are—"whatever God wants." (Don't just accept. God wants *you* to do well. As long as you contribute to your own success, the groundwork is laid. America is the land of opportunity. You have as much right to success as anyone else. It's in your hands, not just God's. God will go along with you when you do the right thing. He gave you the will—remember?)

⮵

It is essential, I think, to recognize these traits in yourself and to use them as a source of encouragement and optimism. But they are merely a foundation. The business edifice, just like a house, needs brick and mortar. You would not say, "Let's put in a window somewhere in the west wall." You'd plan *exactly where.*

So before you even start in business, do your homework—*haz tus tareas.* Read as many books on business success as you can; libraries have whole sections devoted to them. Take business courses at your college or university, or even through the mail. Attend business and marketing seminars.

Then set a clear, definite, *big* goal.

The goal will change as life shapes you. But if it's big enough, the next goal and the next will naturally follow. At first, as you've seen, I wanted to be another Picasso. I did not reach that goal but it led to another: the establishment of a successful art studio. From there I went on to the advertising agency, then to a goal of making a million dollars a year, then to the establishment with my wife of our agency, and now to a dream of living in France, where I'll stay for three years painting and writing. So maybe goal number one will finally come true. (Okay, I won't be another Picasso, but I'll at least be the first Sosa.)

The concept of a "big" goal isn't a difficult one if you switch your thinking from business to love. Remember when you "just knew" you'd found your true love—*el primer amor*? When winning your beloved became an obsession, the only thing that mattered? When if you lost your love you lost everything?

What were the major elements in your quest? Belief, energy, emotion. And what are the major elements in business success? Belief, energy, emotion.

The great Latino artist Jesse Trevino also wanted to be another Picasso. But in the Vietnam War he had his right hand blown off by a land mine. He went into a depression that lasted for two years—and then fought his way out of it. I can still paint, he told himself. He used his left hand to cover the walls of his house with macabre scenes of war, successfully expunging the demons that haunted him and allowing him to go on to other subjects. A giant mural of his (120 by 40 feet) is one of San Antonio's greatest treasures. Like Picasso's work, it will endure for hundreds of years, for hundreds of thousands to enjoy.

⌒

Once your goal is established, write it down—*escríbelo*. This may not be as simple as it sounds, for the goal must "feel right" to you, and you may need a number of versions of it before you come up with exactly what you want. The process may take days or even weeks, but the clearer and more specifically defined the goal is, the more likely you are to achieve it.

The final document should include a clear statement of where you want to be in five years in terms of size, purpose, rate of growth, and gross income and profit. This last is the key, whether you want to manufacture shoes, run a garage, repair watches—or start an advertising agency.

Here, too, there's a formula which I learned only when I sold 49-percent of Sosa, Bromley, Aguilar to DMB&B, a company that had much more experience with profits and reaching profit goals than I did. They believed that you should earn a twenty-percent profit on every dollar of income, and they proved it can be done consistently. Granted, it's difficult at first. However, it is critical in the start-up three years, that you concentrate on showing a profit, period. A twenty-percent profit is a goal that, once your business is running smoothly, you should be able to achieve consistently. After you've done that, you should be able to keep the bulk of these profits for yourself, allocating about one-third to grow your business and to reward your employees with bonuses. DMB&B's twenty-percent goal was above my profit/income ratio when I was on my own. Now I find that the more I stick to it, the easier it becomes to achieve it.

The next most important thing is to make sure you have *a timeline for achievement* of your goal ("by next May, I will get my Master of Business Administration"; "by Jan 1, 2000, I will own my own business"; "by fiscal 2003, I will be making a twenty-percent profit"). Remember that your own salary (before your profit distribution) is part of expenses, just like any other employee's, and should be earned separately from your profits. On the next page, you will find an outline for a written goal for starting your own business.

Once you've finished your plan, read it over three or four times a day—and then, over the next three months, refine it further. Remember: the more specific you can get, the better results you'll have.

⌐

You have more writing to do: a mission statement and a statement reflecting the overall philosophy of your company. *¿Cuál es la filosofía de tu negocio?*

The mission statement should cover two topics: the reason

By ___/___/___ I will own my own business.
(month) (day) (year)

My business will produce/provide _____ for _____ .
(specify products/services) (identify target customer)

a. My business will differ from its competitors by _____ .

b. My business will have a reputation in the industry as _____ .

c. My business will be seen by the public as _____ .

d. My personnel policies will focus on _____ .

e. I will retain primary responsibility for _____ .

f. I will seek to delegate responsibility for _____ .

The company will grow each year and by ___/___/___ (in 5 years) will be
(month) (day) (year)

earning $ _____ in yearly profits.
(any amount)

Personally, I will be earning $ _____ per year in salary and bonuses.
(any amount)

While accomplishing the above, I will set aside no less than 2 hours of quality time each day to contribute to the happiness and well-being of my family and my community.

you're in business and the benefits the business will bring to your clients.

Here's mine for our newly formed company, KJS:

THE KJS MISSION

To help optimize our clients' marketing opportunities by delivering *surprising solutions* to their marketing problems.

It's only fifteen words, but it took us days to write it! Every word is important, every word *means* something, and every associate, every member of the KJS team is expected to master it as soon as he or she joins the firm. Like all mission statements, it gets everyone pointed in the same direction and working toward a common goal.

We have a sister company, Bird in the Hand (my wife Kathy named it), which we recently formed, its purpose being to help our customers keep the clients they already have. We help them find ways to build their customers' loyalty and their own profits by keeping their customers longer, making them happy, and encouraging them to buy more from *them*—not the competition.

THE BIRD-IN-THE-HAND MISSION

To improve our clients' profits by helping them *identify* and *keep* their most valuable customers.

Beyond the mission statement there is also the statement of philosophy, an elaboration of the principles by which we conduct our business. At KJS and Bird in the Hand, this time the statements are identical for both:

THE KJS PHILOSOPHY — *NUESTRA FILOSOFÍA*

We will achieve our mission
1) By having a deep and complete understanding of our clients' customers,
2) By creating the effective, innovative strategies and tactics to get the job done,
3) By designing the most powerful and uncommon advertising

messages that increase our clients' brand awareness and
sales,

4) By delivering these messages in the most efficient way.

Clearly you'll have to shape your own statements to fit the circumstances of your company and the clients you're trying to attract, but this is the essential first step. Your mission statement and
company philosophy are your rallying cry. They tell the world what
you will achieve. They establish your culture, your personality, your
way of doing business. Although there are many companies that
operate without them, they'd be on a surer, faster road to success if
they could only step back and take the time to write these two
"simple" statements—whether they've been in business a month, a
year, a decade, their future would be more assured.

⌐

After you've finished your mission statement and philosophy,
you'll need to prepare a business projection—a statement of annual income and expenses which you will use to guide you
through the entire business year. If you want a bank loan without
a profit-and-loss projection, you have no chance of getting one.
(And, alas, even when Latinos have one, they might have a
tougher time getting that loan than an Anglo would.) No company, no stranger, and few (overly trusting) friends will invest.
And most significantly, you won't be able to run your business ef-
ficiently. You won't know exactly how much income you'll generate. You won't know how to plan your expenses. You won't know
what to pay yourself or your employees. You'll be *guessing* from
month to month, and guessing is a formula for failure.

Yet I am appalled by how many first-time entrepreneurs do not
make their projections. It's not a difficult thing to do. Why would
you want to "take a chance" that all will go well, or spend more on
equipment than you could possibly make back in income? Why
would you imagine that clients "surely" exist without knowing
that they really do? All you need is a solid, realistic projection.

There are many ways of writing up a projection (see example
on page 175). I've seen some that go on for ten pages. Yours

PROJECTIONS FOR COMPANY ABC   YEAR _____

A INCOME — Where the business comes from (your clients)

B TOTAL BILLINGS — Total of monies coming in each month

C OVERHEAD — Your fixed overhead, salaries, rent, etc.

D OTHER EXPENSES — Nonrecurring expenditures needed to do business each month

E NEW BUSINESS — Expenditures to help get more business

F TOTAL EXPENSES — Total of monies going out

G Profit or loss

H How are we doin' so far?

CLIENT	JAN	FEB	MAR	APR	MAY	JUN	JUL	AUG	SEP	OCT	NOV	DEC
A	25,000	25,000	25,000	25,000	25,000	25,000	25,000	25,000	25,000	25,000	25,000	25,000
B	20,000	20,000	20,000	20,000	20,000	20,000	20,000	20,000	20,000	20,000	20,000	20,000
C	15,000	15,000	15,000	15,000	15,000	15,000	15,000	15,000	15,000	15,000	15,000	15,000
D	10,000	10,000	10,000	10,000	10,000	10,000	10,000	10,000	10,000	10,000	10,000	10,000
E	10,000	10,000	10,000	10,000	10,000	10,000	10,000	10,000	10,000	10,000	10,000	10,000
F	5,000	5,000	5,000	5,000	5,000	5,000	5,000	5,000	5,000	5,000	5,000	5,000
G	5,000	5,000	5,000	5,000	5,000	5,000	5,000	5,000	5,000	5,000	5,000	5,000
H	2,000	2,000	2,000	2,000	2,000	2,000	2,000	2,000	2,000	2,000	2,000	2,000
TOTAL BILLING BY MONTH	92,000	X 12	= 1,104,000									
TOTAL FIXED OVERHEAD BY MONTH	64,600	X 12	= 775,200									
VARIABLE EXPENSES	5,000	X 12	= 60,000									
NEW BUSINESS EXPENSES	4,000	X 12	= 48,000									
TOTAL MONTHLY EXPENSES	73,600	X 12	= 883,200									
PROFIT BEFORE TAXES & INCENTIVE COMPENSATION	18,400	X 12	= 220,800									
CUMULATIVE PROFIT OR LOSS	18,400	36,800	55,200 ETC.									

20% PROFIT

probably won't be that elaborate, but the more detail you include, the better. Essentially, you should *as accurately as possible* set forth:

- Where your business will come from
- How much money your client or customer will pay you each month
- How much you will pay out per month in *fixed* expenses—salaries, rent, interest on a loan if any, insurance, telephone, office supplies, etc.—expenses that will be there every month regardless of how much money comes in
- How much you will pay on average in *variable* expenses per month—outlays you can control and vary according to the business volume you do—expenses to attract new business (e.g., preparation of brochures), buying materials and parts to be able to complete the product, and the like.

The total monthly expenses, fixed and variable, should come to eighty percent of the total monthly income. This is critical, because the remaining 20 percent is your profit. If your projected expenses are over 80 percent, you'll have to find a way to cut. (As noted, at the beginning of your venture the formula doesn't have to hold so stringently. You can go for six months or even twelve at break-even or slightly better just to get started. From time to time you may even project losses in any given month, but you must project a profit every quarter.)

A hint: Leave *all* your profits in the business for the first three to five years in case of unexpected turbulence. You don't want to have to borrow from a bank (or borrow *more* from a bank) to cover unexpected costs at the beginning.

Now it's time to write the actual business plan: ten steps in all. My outline is simpler than most you'll find elsewhere, but it does the job.

You'll want to cover:

1. History, background, and trends in your business
2. A review of the current situation, including a detailed analysis of the competition
3. Opportunities and areas for growth
4. Your singular goal
5. Your market, both geographical and psychological, in depth (know your customer!)
6. Main strategies (big ideas) for reaching your goal (no more than twelve, for it blurs focus; no fewer than six, for at least some alternatives are essential)
7. One to three specific actions you can take to implement each strategy
8. Assignment of responsibilities and deadlines for each action
9. Your budget
10. Your measurement of success
11. Refinement for continued success

The primary purpose of this book is not, of course, to teach you how to write a business plan; many other business books go into far greater detail. But most can be simplified to my outline. And the simpler the better.

Be sure to review your plan every three months, making additions and deletions as circumstances warrant. In implementing it, remain flexible. A business plan is a living document. You must control its breathing.

Most business failures occur because the above steps are not instituted. You'd be amazed at the figures. Of all new businesses started in the United States every year, ninety-five percent fail—*and ninety-five percent of them did not start out with a clear goal, a mission statement, an accurate projection, or a solid plan.* Follow my methods, and I promise you'll be well ahead of those ominous statistics.

↪

As you grow, you'll find your projections changing—they'll be going up—and your business plans becoming sharper. *"Más lo haces,*

SIMPLE BUSINESS PLAN

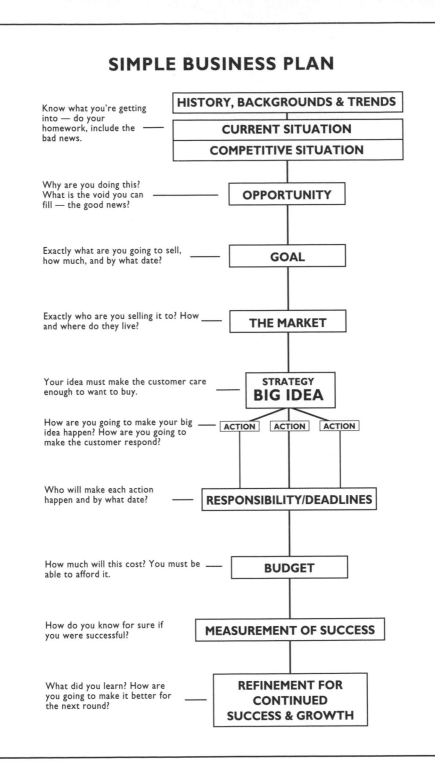

Know what you're getting into — do your homework, include the bad news.

HISTORY, BACKGROUNDS & TRENDS

CURRENT SITUATION

COMPETITIVE SITUATION

Why are you doing this? What is the void you can fill — the good news?

OPPORTUNITY

Exactly what are you going to sell, how much, and by what date?

GOAL

Exactly who are you selling it to? How and where do they live?

THE MARKET

Your idea must make the customer care enough to want to buy.

**STRATEGY
BIG IDEA**

How are you going to make your big idea happen? How are you going to make the customer respond?

ACTION   **ACTION**   **ACTION**

Who will make each action happen and by what date?

RESPONSIBILITY/DEADLINES

How much will this cost? You must be able to afford it.

BUDGET

How do you know for sure if you were successful?

MEASUREMENT OF SUCCESS

What did you learn? How are you going to make it better for the next round?

**REFINEMENT FOR
CONTINUED
SUCCESS & GROWTH**

más fácil es"—the more you do it, the easier it gets. You'll be better able to predict the future, to sense trends, to anticipate pitfalls.

Your own job description will change, too. As you grow, you'll be turning over the daily running of the business to your employees while you concentrate on the "grand strategy," the long-range plans, the innovations that will continue to help your business grow. You will concentrate on hiring well, on giving your people respect, trusting them and training them, all the while realizing that they need room to develop their own methods.

The chart on page 180 shows you the development of the maturing manager as the business grows with him or her.

At first, you'll devote 75 percent of your time to hands-on work in the business, 23 percent to acquiring new business, and 2 percent to planning for the future. In the middle stages, you'll be doing the daily tasks only 35 percent of the time, spending 30 percent on training your people, 25 percent on acquiring new business, and 10 percent on future planning. (This is a tough period for the manager, since you must learn to give up total control and rely more on others to get the job done.) The mature manager (and I've finally reached that mixed-blessings status: I like the position but not the age it represents) will spend 50 percent of his time on developing his employees, 25 percent attracting new business, and the rest on community service, reinforcing relationships with current clients, refining plans, and—very occasionally—doing a little hands-on "work."

The established business is self-sustaining, beyond the direct control of the *jefe*. The entrepreneur who has planned carefully and followed those plans with prudence and imagination can expect to become a successful (and wealthy) businessperson.

∽

Three final thoughts before I turn to how to market your business to your clients and to the world:

1. Don't give up if things go poorly at first. *Nunca para, sigue, sigue.* Latinos are particularly vulnerable to setbacks. Initial defeat too often brings back to us our fears of being unworthy, of thinking we've run into prejudice, of attributing our

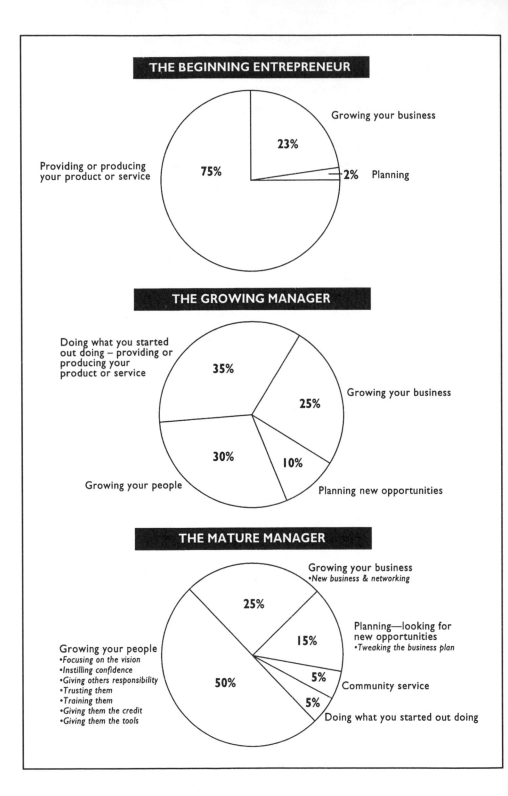

THE BEGINNING ENTREPRENEUR

Growing your business

23%

Providing or producing
your product or service

75%

2% Planning

THE GROWING MANAGER

Doing what you started
out doing – providing or
producing your
product or service

35%

Growing your business

25%

30%

10%

Growing your people

Planning new opportunities

THE MATURE MANAGER

Growing your business
•New business & networking

25%

15%

Planning—looking for
new opportunities
•Tweaking the business plan

Growing your people
•Focusing on the vision
•Instilling confidence
•Giving others responsibility
•Trusting them
•Training them
•Giving them the credit
•Giving them the tools

50%

5%

Community service

5%

Doing what you started out doing

bad start to "God's will" that we not succeed. But keep fighting! If you are sure in your vision, your goals will emerge
clearer than ever and your plans will be even more accurate. What you see is what you'll eventually achieve.

2. Don't burn out. Overwork can be ruinous. If you feel yourself getting tired, if ideas no longer leap into your head, or
if getting to work seems a struggle, take time off. Relax. Re-
fresh yourself. Even if you think you can't afford the time.

3. Don't stay where you are; you're losing ground. This, too, is
a trap we can fall into. Maybe we're as yet so unused to
success—so surprised by it—that once it's achieved we celebrate. And keep *on* celebrating. And don't try for more. In
my case, there was a two-year period during which I relied
on former projections and did not set new goals. I relished
my success so long, I actually *forgot* to set new goals. So nothing happened. Things began to stagnate. If the stagnation
had continued, the business might have failed.

CHAPTER 14

MARKETING YOUR COMPANY

¡Y tú también!

Latinos who are new in business are often seen as being a step behind their competition. That is why, for us, marketing is particularly important. We must be more aggressive, more creative, more innovative. We must have confidence coursing through our veins, for confidence is a superb marketing tool. (If you think you're the best, others will.) We must announce loudly and clearly to our customers and clients that ours is a solid company, that it will pay rewards to do business with us, that precisely *because* we're Latinos we've had to fight harder and learn more and therefore are superb colleagues. Assertive, not retiring. Optimistic, not pessimistic. Positive, not negative. We *are* as good at business as anyone else. Without that inner belief, it will be difficult to market your company to the world.

∽

Okay. You've conceived of a fine business and made the right plans for its success. But how will it succeed if nobody hears about it? How will people understand how good you—or your product—are if they don't know you exist?

Marketing your company takes the same kind of planning as *creating* your company. And it takes the same kind of plan.

1. Your objective must be clearly stated.
2. Your competition must be analyzed in depth.
3. Your strategies for selling your product or implementing your services must be specifically defined.
4. Your actions must be set forth in as detailed a fashion as possible.

The difference here is that the reader of this material will not be yourself but your customer. Yes, as you are writing your business plan, you are in effect writing an advertisement for yourself or your product. Here, you are not planning to create a product or to manufacture it, but rather to sell it.

⌐⌐

To sell your product, you must first consider the five basic elements of marketing:

- Product—what it is you are selling
- Place—where you will sell it
- Packaging—what it will look like
- Price—how much it will cost the buyer or user
- Promotion—how you will get it recognized

To these famous "five p's" I've added a vital sixth: personal. Knowing your customer, knowing how to best "touch" him or her, and finally knowing how to *keep* the customers—especially the most valuable customers—you win.

In *The One to One Future*, Don Peppers and Martha Rogers observe that today Americans sell to the world under an old but simple philosophy: We Make, You Buy. For years, the U.S. had produced the dominant products on the market, and foreign nations longed to emulate American know-how. It was almost as if we could strong-arm our customers into buying what we sold, no matter what its quality or uniqueness. We made little effort to find out to whom we were selling, for it made little difference. They were buying; why did we have to know who they were?

That's not the way things will be in the near future; indeed, I don't think that's the way things are now. I believe all companies are going to have to focus on their customers far more than they have in the past—and the way to focus is by getting personal, by knowing your customers almost as intimately as they know themselves.

∽

There are eight things you must know before you start marketing your company.

1. *Know yourself.* Know that your product is sound or your service invaluable. Know you're at least as good as anyone else. Know you're the best.

2. *Know what you want your company to be.* What is it that you will call success?

Today, Kathy and I want to build an agency quite different from "the biggest." At Sosa, Bromley, Aguilar, we were shooting to build a hundred-million-dollar business, and we did it. Now we want an agency half that size—hardly an insignificant sum, but small compared to my earlier company.

Why such a modest goal? First, because it will allow me to earn about the same profits as a company twice the size. After thirty years in the business, I've learned to be many times more efficient than I was when I started. Through strategic planning, I can anticipate problems and opportunities I couldn't see before. And I pass all my learning to the younger people in our organization. In turn, *they* are more efficient: they do more in less time, and they do better quality work with more confidence. A smaller company will also allow me personal contacts with all my clients; I'll be able to plan advertising strategies with them and help design strong communication strategies and programs. And it will let me do something I've come to love: teach the young on our staff to be the best. I want to leave a legacy not only of competence and professionalism but of real innovation. I want to see ideas I plant grown and transformed by others in ways I cannot yet visualize. And finally, I want to spend time with my family, build a closer relationship with my older children—and spend time in France, Mexico, Spain, and Italy, painting.

So my company is different—*los tiempos cambian*—but it's the one I want it to be. And I measure its success not only monetarily but by the freedom it gives me.

3. Know whom you want to beat. Who is your main competitor?

If business is a "war" (and in many ways it is) then it is important to create an "enemy"—somebody to beat and defeat. August Busch, for example, got motivated to make Anheuser Busch the world's leading brewery when the Miller Brewing Company brought out the "killer instinct" in him. Miller was spending fifty million dollars a year in advertising, Anheuser Busch a little less. Then Miller threw out a challenge: "We're number one and we're getting bigger while Anheuser Busch shrinks." That was the statement that started the biggest beer war this country had ever seen. Miller was the enemy and August Busch was on the warpath.

Busch *doubled* the advertising ante to a hundred million, an unheard-of amount twenty years ago. It did the job. In three years, Budweiser replaced Miller High Life as the number one beer in the country. And all because Miller became the enemy and Anheuser Busch had a *cause* greater than selling a lot of beer, greater than just making a profit.

Obviously, we're talking huge stakes here; you're not going to copy Busch. But the principle is the same: identify your competition and make them the enemy. Through whatever legal means are at your disposal, including hiring away their best people, go after them.

4. Know your customer inside out.

This goes back to what I said about personalizing your marketing. In the early eighties Kit Goldsbury bought Pace Picante Sauce from David Pace. The salsa had been produced in one shop out of three huge vats, with five women hand-filling bottles of the Mexican hot sauce. The firm was quite successful. Mr. Pace had managed to convince supermarkets that his salsa deserved a place on their shelves, and since it was the best quality around, the supermarkets accommodated him. As far as Mr. Pace was concerned, the supermarkets were his clients—after all, *they* were the ones who bought the stuff from him. He never saw the need to court anyone other than supermarket buyers and managers.

Kit had a different idea. He wanted to reach the person who *ate* the salsa, the actual customer, the shopper who physically took the salsa from the supermarket shelves. So he conducted focus groups and individual interviews to discover the basic information about his customers: their level of education, their gender, their income, where they lived, worked, played, and shopped. Most important, he wanted to know *what went on in their minds*. What influenced them? Why did they choose Pace's or his competition's salsa? How did they use it? How did they feel about it as a brand? By so knowing the mind of the customer he was able to tailor his advertising messages, choose the right media, conduct the best point-of-sale campaigns. His business grew first regionally, then nationally, then internationally. Salsa sales became bigger than catsup sales (just as nacho sales at baseball games are bigger now than hot dog sales). Two years ago Kit sold Pace's to Campbell Soup for $1.1 *billion*. Not bad for a man who bought three large vats of Mexican hot sauce.

His strategy should be yours. No matter whether you're trying to attract a single client, a small group of buyers, or as many consumers as you can get, the more you know them the better you'll be able to reach them—*lo mejor que conoces al cliente, lo más que le vendes*. And reaching people is what marketing is all about.

5. Know how you are different from your competition.

Your mission statement and statement of philosophy should include the reasons you're different from the competition. At KJS, remember, we make a strong point of discovering critical information about our clients' consumers—we'll research how they feel and how they think. We believe we do this better than any of our competition, so we hit it hard. For Columbia, for example, we discovered through focus groups that the two things that afflict people most when they have to go to an emergency room are fear and pain. So our advertising will address those concerns: "Columbia will do everything possible to ease the fear and pain people feel." We also discovered that people expect hospitals to be the "protectors" of life, to have an almost Godlike quality. This insight led us to this strategic message: "God is the giver of life. Columbia is the protector of life."

There are other areas in which we're different from our competition beyond helping our clients better understand the consumer, and at all times we *write down* our strengths; our face to our clients is as important as theirs is to their customers.

First of all, we look for surprising solutions to marketing problems.

For example, for the internationally known cosmetics company Maybelline, we interviewed dozens of women about makeup. In focus groups, the moderator, Pat Parea, put a situation to ponder before twelve of them.

"When do you use makeup?" she asked.

"When we go out to work or a social event" was the answer.

"When do you *not* use makeup?"

"When we're at home, especially cleaning up, vacuuming. Kicking back, stuff like that."

"Now," Pat continued, "suppose you're at home, vacuuming, no makeup on, and suddenly you remember you've forgotten something you need from the supermarket down the street. You dash out without makeup and run to the store. All of a sudden, walking down the aisle with your shopping cart, you see a very important person whom you know coming toward you. What would you do?"

All twelve women, in unison, shielded their faces with their hands. "Oh no!"

"I'd turn around quickly, go to another aisle," said one.

"I'd hide," said another.

"I'd leave the cart there and run out of the store," said a third.

Pat asked for an explanation. "Are you ashamed of how you look?"

"No, but I wouldn't feel like myself without makeup."

"You mean you need makeup in order to feel whole? That without makeup you aren't you?"

"No . . . not exactly. *But without makeup I'm not the me I want the world to see.*"

"Wow!" I said, having overheard it all.

What led to the insight was very astute questioning from the moderator, but also observation of the group's body language.

From the critical consumer insight came this marketing strategy: *With Maybelline You're the You for All the World to See.*

A surprising solution?

Yes. In this case, surprising in its simplicity.

There are other ways we're different from our competition.

- We translate insights into sound marketing strategies—we're marketing strategists first and doers next.
- Our creative product sells!
- We can help our clients keep their customers, not just get them.

As you see, I'm not being reticent. I'm marketing.

Making sure your prospective client understands how you are better and different from the competition is critical. Many times clients talk to so many people that by the time they are ready to make a decision all presentations seem alike. Make them remember you by making yourself distinctive. Being different is being memorable. They won't hire you if they don't remember you.

6. Know your philosophy statement and display it for all to see.

At Sosa, Bromley, Aguilar and Noble (now Bromley Aguilar), each person had the statement of philosophy on his or her desk, and there is a gigantic poster detailing it in the lobby. The agency's overall beliefs—that good advertising begins with startling, innovative ideas; that it captures the heart and mind; that we are partners of our clients, not servants or clones; that we perform with passion and courage; that we are able to look into the future, beyond the expected—beyond the horizon—are woven into that philosophy and it is unique to that agency. But a sound philosophy statement is common to all good businesses: it lays a platform for action, a foundation from which deviation is possible but radical changes are unnecessary.

You are the one to set this philosophy for the company. You must write it, then teach it to your team, "market" it to your colleagues and then to your clients. The business should reflect your ideas and your personality. This is essential. For you are a leader,

Agency Philosophy

The Startling Innovative Idea.
A surprising solution to a marketing problem.

We must first have the talent to recognize it.
Even when it appears raw, as ore.
Before the world sees it for what it is. Gold.

To recognize such an idea we must listen well. To each other.
To our client. And to the ultimate expert, our consumer.

We must believe the idea will make people care.
We must believe it will make people respond. So that we can
stand up for it. With passion. And courage.

The idea must motivate us to produce outstanding communications.
That will work magic. That will capture the heart.
The mind. And the imagination.

We're marketing partners. Not ad makers.
We're strategists. Not clones.

That's why we will challenge. That's why we will startle.
That's why we will think big...
Beyond the Horizon. Beyond the Expected.

Sosa
Bromley
Aguilar &
Associates

and a leader has vision and the ability to impart that vision to others.

7. Know how to build a culture and teach it.

Every company has its "culture." It may be a culture of chaos, with papers flying in every direction and workers rushing about without real destinations; it may be so carefully managed that innovation and worker participation is discouraged; it may be smoothly run, yet allow for new ideas, dissent, and idiosyncrasy. A company's culture takes time to develop, as the leader gets footing and the team get comfortable with what's expected of them. Most businesses don't have a completely clear direction when they start (the business plan notwithstanding); cohesiveness grows as the business does. But I have four suggestions for building a solid culture. They've worked for me and they'll work for you.

- Promote a culture of strategic thinkers, of people who are self-motivated, people who think and plan ahead. Lead them, but don't ask them to follow blindly. Teach your people to focus on finding solutions to problems, not just identifying them.

- Foster open communication. Keep your door open as well as your mind. Remember that everyone in your organization is an important contributor to your success, and that people brainstorming together generate magnificent ideas.

- Build a culture of teachers and students, with you serving as the foremost example. Encourage your senior people to help the younger ones. Foster trust and empathy. The less jealousy, the less fear of "someone taking my job," the more cooperativeness in a common cause, the more productive the business will be.

- Involve everybody in your "culture" in the decision-making process, even if they're not directly involved in the discussions. At the least, explain to everyone, even the most junior staff members, why you've made the decisions you have. Of course the final decisions rest with you—that's why you earn the lion's share of the profits! But when the whole team contributes, creativity flourishes, and the business will thrive.

"I thought this was a chapter on marketing my company," you might say. "I haven't heard much about it yet."

Well, actually you have, for by following the eight points discussed in this chapter (the eighth is below), you'll be able to establish a business with something more than just a product or service to sell. It really starts with selling yourself, and selling yourself is perhaps the best marketing strategy of all.

"How is this different for Latinos than for Anglos?" might be another question.

The answer is that there's no difference. Any good business, Latino as well as Anglo, will have strong leadership building a strong culture. No racial or ethnic limitations and no bias should come into play.

8. Know how the big boys and girls do it.

There's much to be learned from the giants. For purposes of this book, and for our own business, we've researched a lot of corporate leaders, and while they have millions (even billions) of dollars to spend on marketing and you may have only a few hundred or a few thousand, there's much you can copy from what they do. They have made their products "brand names." When you think of fast food, you think of McDonald's; when you think of jeans, you think of Levi's; when you think of athletic shoes, you think of Nike; when you think of soft drinks, you think of Coke. These world-famous brands have three things in common.

- First, they commit as much in resources (time as well as money) to their *image* as they do to the quality of their products or services. This is why their products are "brand names." In a smaller way, you must try to make your own product or service so familiar to *your* market that when customers go out looking for the kind of product you make, they will think of you.

- Second, they are spectacularly good at differentiating themselves from the competition.

- Third and perhaps most important, they link their product or service to a powerful human emotion.

This last point is vital. Many corporations advertise differently to Anglos and Latinos. The *very* biggest, however, concentrate on emotion over practicality in all cases.

Take the (copyrighted) pyramids shown opposite. You'll see immediately that the actual product is at the base of the communications pyramid, the product's benefit is next highest, in the middle, and the universal human value is at the very top. As an example of the potency of this approach, I was recently at a soccer game played by fifth-graders. After the game, one of the fathers told the victorious team he would take them to McDonald's to celebrate—and a different father told the losing team that he would take them to McDonald's to cheer them up! Talk about family values! McDonald's "top of the pyramid" positioning has convinced the kids that Ronald might be there and convinced the adults that they will be a better mommy or daddy (or grandparent) if they take the child to McDonald's. Awesome!

These companies—and the products they produce—capture our minds with universal *emotional* themes that everyone can relate to. They do it brilliantly. Imagine—a beverage made of carbonated water, sugar, caffeine, and a syrup flavoring can stand for world harmony. The "real thing"? Yes, in the sense that a deity is the real thing—more powerful than all others—in Coke's case so much more powerful that it seems hard to equate the product with the message. Yet we do.

What we can learn from the "big boys" is that the more distinctive you can make your product, the better your chances of selling it; the more targeted and original your service, the better your chances of attracting clients. But obviously most of us don't have the millions of dollars necessary to make our products or services household names, or to give them the aura of universality shared by Coke and Nike. Indeed, we sometimes only have a few dollars to spend on marketing, and sometimes nothing at all.

This doesn't mean you can't market or shouldn't try. Quite the contrary! Millions of people have started successful businesses on a shoestring, while millions of dollars have been "blown" on trying to market businesses that should never have been started in the first place.

The best marketing strategy for even the smallest business is to

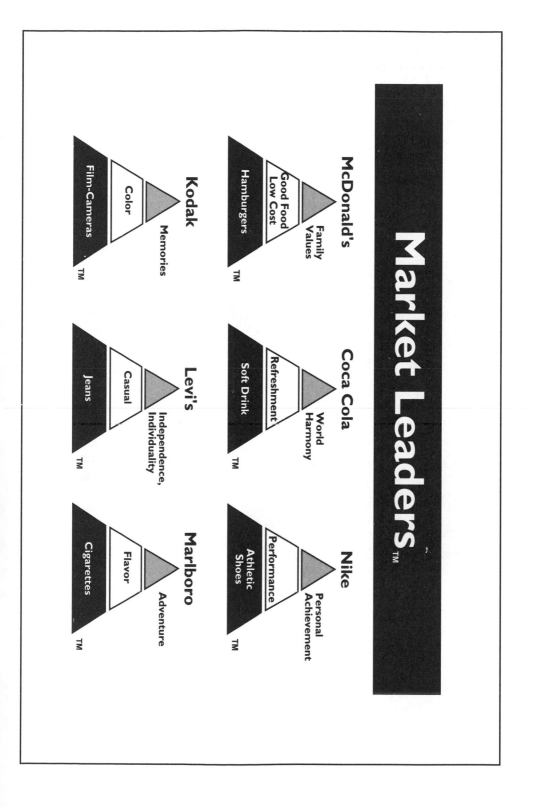

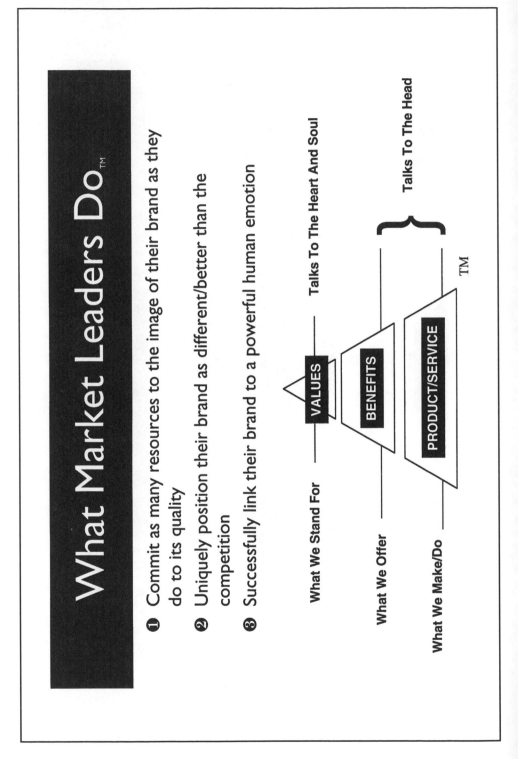

produce a product or supply a service that is better, cheaper, or faster than the competition's. That's a given. Second, you must have a Unique Selling Proposition, a simple statement of *why* your product or service is the one to choose. ("Open 24 Hours a Day," "Free Delivery to All Parts of the City," "All You Can Eat for $9.95," "Color Printing Throughout" are simple, familiar examples of USPs.) Third, at the very least you must print brochures or flyers describing your product or service, make sure they are mailed to or displayed at places where people likely to want what you supply are located—and use them to tell your local newspaper when you've started a new business. Fourth, you must aggressively talk up your business everywhere you can—among friends, by contacting prospective clients, by attending conventions and sales meetings, etc.

Most important, however, you must give what you do a "personality." It's not a coincidence that so many businesses from restaurants to beauty salons to auto-repair shops proudly proclaim themselves as "Pete's Place" or "Chez Susan" or "Roberto's." These owners are saying to the world, "I stand behind what I do; you can count on me; if you have complaints you know who's to blame and if you have compliments you know whom to praise." You are the best advertisement—the best marketing tool—for your own business, and if you do not stand for and speak up for what you do, who else will?

Capital, then, is not essential to good marketing—surely not as essential as a good idea, an aggressive approach, a winning smile, and the careful building of trust, doing what you say you'll do. I started with a pencil, a drawing pad, and a homemade desk in a tin toolshed (less than a hundred-dollar investment), and I aggressively "marketed" what I had to offer: my talent. Pete Cortez bought a five-table restaurant for fifty bucks, served good food, made sure that his community knew of the quality and low price, and transformed it into San Antonio's biggest and most popular Mexican restaurant, Mi Tierra.

There are many examples of people who built businesses with no capital but a knack for promotion. Suzie Garcia, a Cuban woman in her early twenties, saved a few hundred dollars and with her husband started a small coffeeshop called Espuma's in

San Antonio's historical section. She used her money to rent and restore an old house, served the best coffee she could find, added a section where customers could buy a variety of newspapers and enjoy art exhibits by local artists. In effect she made her shop into a kind of neighborhood clubhouse, a place where people discuss local issues, post ads on her bulletin board, relax and feel comfortable. Her shop is as busy as the most crowded Starbuck's, but with one vital thing more to offer—Suzy's personality.

Or take the case of Guillermo Lozano, a popular radio personality for twenty years who suddenly found himself out of a job at the age of forty-five. He then became station manager of a new Spanish-language "romantic" station, but a new owner transformed it into an English-language "easy listening" station and Guillermo was jobless again. He had no paycheck, but he had himself and a knowledge of radio. Armed with a pencil and pad, he made the rounds of every ad agency in Texas. "I'll translate your ads into Spanish. I'll *write* your Spanish ads. I'll do the Spanish voice-overs. I'll be the on-camera talent." In less than a year he had made himself indispensable. Today, twenty years later, he is not thinking of retirement; he is one of the busiest, happiest people in the growing Hispanic media market.

There's a small Hispanic-owned bank in Miami, so small it has zero dollars for advertising. In no way can it compete with the big boys and girls by trying traditional TV and radio advertising—so it does what it does best: targets only Hispanic-owned businesses. Working through the local Chamber of Commerce, its three officers acquired a list of all Latino-owned businesses in the greater Miami area. They divided the list among themselves and made it a goal for each to call on two businesses a day with this simple proposition: "Do you need money to grow your business? We'd like to help."

"Of course we need money. Come on in!" the business owners said.

No "regular" bank makes this kind of approach to Latino small business owners, and of course not every prospect qualified for a loan. But the bank is building a quality loan portfolio by making smart loans to a market the competition ignored.

I've said that to market your budding company well, you must market yourself. This doesn't necessarily mean you must "go public," but those in your company and the clients you service must know you and what you stand for.

Before you read this book, you may not have known that Roberto Goizueta was the CEO of Coca-Cola or Herb Kelleher of Southwest Airlines. They are not household names. (Bill Gates is an important exception; he *is* Microsoft.) Yet these two men have powerful, commanding personalities to match their vision and their executive abilities—as, I think, do the heads of all truly successful companies.

What happens when charismatic leaders retire or are replaced? It depends. If people who are good managers but have no leadership skills (and there are many) take over, the business will grow at a slower pace, flatten out, or begin to lose momentum and sales. If good leaders succeed good leaders (as in the case of Coca-Cola, for example, when Goizueta replaced Woodruff), then the new leader, building on the groundwork of his predecessor, will make the company grow even larger and stronger.

Often, of course, individuals market themselves *to* the public. This is true in the case of athletes, performers, writers, and artists. The three tenors, for example, are fabulous salesmen for—the three tenors. The guests on *The Tonight Show* or *Oprah* are selling themselves more than the books they've written or the movies in which they're about to appear. In essence, the name *becomes* the product. Many people don't go to the opera, they go to hear Domingo; some people don't see a basketball game, they see Michael Jordan.

Paloma Picasso is a fine example of someone who markets herself to market her products. She *always* looks perfect. She has abundant style, travels in the "right" social circles, often features herself in advertisements for her cosmetics and jewelry, and personally sells to the great jewelry stores like Tiffany's.

She has two other assets. Her father's name and her tremendous talent.

Someone without a national "name" yet is the fashion designer Veronica Prida. Hoping to rise to the level of the internationally known (and self-marketing) Oscar de la Renta, she told me this:

"I want what I wear to be what I represent. The way I promote is how I look. So I go out to a lot of activities, a lot of parties. I am a public person. I do several things to make sure that my fashions are seen and that newspaper articles are written about me.

"I do fashion benefits that get a lot of people who buy expensive dresses involved. Once in a while, I *give* someone a piece of my work so they can be surprised and talk it over with their friends. I develop good public relations with the press. I send them stuff. I call them, check with them. They become my personal friends. I want them to know that I am there for them and don't just call them when I need them.

"I promote the fashion *category*, not just me. I promote fashion and style."

Not a bad formula for anyone in any profession.

⏤

It's most urgent to market your business well when you're trying to attract new business, to sell a new product, or to win over a potential client. All my life I've taken particular care in the preparation of new business presentations, and I'll end the chapter by showing you, verbatim, our overall presentation plan.

Adapt it to your own business, your own company. The details will vary, but the overall principles remain constant. Use it wisely, and you'll have taken a major step toward success.

Presentation Check List
(what they should see)

1. List of client's people
2. List of our people
3. Meeting date, time, place, room, materials needed
4. How we're different
5. Goal
6. Target audience

7. Target markets
8. Research findings
9. Communication pyramid
10. Consumer insight
11. Overall strategic direction
12. Creative brief
13. Gotta do's
14. Creative copy
15. Collateral/Promotions/PR
16. Customer retention
17. Media
18. Budgets
19. Timelines
20. Responsibilities
21. How we measure success

This Is What We Ask Our People to Do
Before the Presentation

What we do before the presentation is as important as the presentation itself. This is the time to get to know the client and what he's looking for.

So ask the prospective client as many questions as you like:
• Who are the decision makers?
• What are their goals?
• What is their history?
• Who is their competition?

You'll find they'll tell you a lot. Call them and visit with them in person as often as necessary. Collect all their research. Remember, they *want* to hire someone—why not us? Start the "bonding" process.

Make sure the entire agency is aware of the prospective client's visit to your offices. A day or two prior to your presentation, alert the agency about the visit. Dress for success on the day of the presentation, and extend your usual hospitality and professionalism.

Talk to their consumer. Conduct focus groups—tape them. Get the consumer insight. This may be the single most important thing you do.

In sum, know more about their consumer than they know.

On the Day of the Presentation

1. *Welcome them with a sign in the lobby.* Make sure their logo is on it.

2. *Have refreshments and snacks available as they come into your offices/meeting room.* Suggest removal of coats for informality. Get comfortable. Chat about personal stuff before getting into the actual pitch.

3. *Ask your agency's new business team leader to welcome prospective client and give an overview of what the agency has done to prepare for the meeting.*

4. *Make short introductions of agency people.*

5. *Ask client to introduce their people, giving short backgrounds. This helps break the ice—makes the setting friendlier.*

6. *Be bold!* Remember, they need you as much as you need them. They *want* to buy. Assume the sale.

7. *Entertain.* The client, in this case, is the consumer.

8. *Build your presentation around a surprising solution to their marketing problem.*

9. *Assume a leadership position*—be No. 1 in intelligence, creativity, strategy, etc.

Examples: We have

- Looked into the opportunity for you
- Talked to your consumers
- Talked to your wholesalers (if applicable)
- Talked to your retailers

- Insight into your customers
- Insight into your competition
- Strategic thinking to share with you

- A point-of-view of the opportunity
- An estimate of the sales increases you can expect
- A method we use to turn all this into sales.

But first . . .
10. *Ask them these questions:*

- If you were to describe the ideal company you want to hire, what qualities would it have?

- What are the five main characteristics that you look for in that company?

11. *Encourage conversation—not "presentation" dialogue. Keep them talking about themselves.* What ads do they like? Why? Who are the marketers they admire most? Why? This is the chance to begin to build trust.

12. *While they are talking, observe and determine the power people (both formal and informal), the decision makers.* What do their titles and positions mean? Who's friendly? Who will be tough? Why?

13. *Present overview of opportunity:*

- The market demographic psychographics
- The category and its history of growth with analysis of why and how it's grown
- Product usage, incidence, etc.
- Share of market and $ value of share
- Results of research (taped and well edited focus groups work great)
- Conclusions
- Discussion (encourage dialogue at all stages)

14. *Never apologize.* Don't say "I'm sorry we didn't have enough time to accomplish this or that." Show them what you have, not what you don't.

15. *Present a list of what makes you attractive.* Suggest to them: You should hire us because—

- You like the way we think
- You want the best creative talents
- You demand superior service
- You want passion in your business, etc.

16. *Present a list of what makes them attractive.* Tell them: we want your business because—

- We believe in your product
- You represent a milestone in our history
- We love the challenge, etc.

17. *Give them more than they asked for.* They are as interested in your strategic thinking as in your creative.

18. *Now, and only now, start talking about yourself.* Give one to three short case histories to illustrate the agency's talent in client's category with "Startling Innovative" examples of advertising, promotions, media, direct marketing, etc.

19. *Show examples of the work we've done for other clients.*

20. *Give short history of our company, growth, philosophy (15 minutes max).*

21. *Present the people who would work on the business.* This shows that, "We've thought of who will handle your account—here they are—we're ready to go to work tomorrow."

22. *Be visionary.* Share your vision on the industry, the market, their product, your agency.

23. *Ask for the order.*

24. *Be confident.* Talk to the prospect like you've been partners for years.

25. *Discuss next steps and timeline.*

26. *Leave time for questions and answers—about 30 minutes.*

After the Presentation

1. *Follow up with letters, notes, telephone calls and personal visits.*

2. *Keep talking after the presentation.* This dialogue before and after the formal pitch is critical to success. Others don't do it. They will like your tenacity. Talk every other day or so until the decision is made.

3. *When the call comes in to announce you've won, smile!* Dance! Shout! You've deserved the win!

CHAPTER 15

THE RIGHT PLACE—THE RIGHT TIME—THE RIGHT GENERATION

Mañana is today

The most recent census figures, as reported in the *New York Times*, point out a number of troubling trends.

- Average household income for Latinos has dropped 14 percent, from $26,000 to $22,900, since 1989.
- In 1995, income rose for all ethnic groups except Latinos.
- Latinos make up 10 percent of this country's population— and comprise 25 percent of the nation's poor.

Social scientists and statisticians believe three factors influence these figures:

1. Structural changes in the economy that have reduced the number of blue-collar jobs
2. The high Latino dropout rate from high school, compounding the failure of institutions at every educational level to teach marketable skills
3. Employers who see Latin immigrants—particularly those

who speak poor English—as "disposable workers" fit only
for part-time jobs

Are Latinos, they ask, destined to become an entrenched underclass? Will we always be the "working poor"?

The social scientists and statisticians have not dug deeply
enough. What they say might be true, but if that were all, then we
would be truly in danger. We must, I'm sure, look beneath the
surface of economic and societal conditions to find the explanation for the statistics. We must look to—and *face up* to—the
Latino mind-set for the answer. Once we recognize it, we can
change.

Indeed, the change is already well under way.

⤶

The Mexican essayist and philosopher Octavio Paz speaks of the
mexicano enano—the Mexican dwarf. We've been "dwarfed," he
says, because we are the children of the *conquistadores* and the
Indian women whom they mercilessly violated. *Somos hijos de la
chingada*—we are the sons and daughters of that rape; we are bas-
tards. And like it or not, it is this mind-set, established generations ago—the attitudes I have described as our "cultural
shackles"—that keep us subservient, prevent us from achieving as
we should.

I know it's not polite to agree with Paz. I know that I'll be accused of fostering the stereotype. I know I often won't be believed. I know that few of us *want* to believe.

Of course you have every right to disagree—what Paz and I are
saying is heavy wood. I know it's easier (and preferable) not to
blame ourselves for our relative lack of success but to blame society, "others," prejudice, bias, "the system."

But this attitude says, in effect, "There's nothing we can do
about it. No matter how hard we try, society will beat us down."
And if you've been with me so far, you'll know that my answer is
a resounding "No!" We don't have to be forever locked into
our mind-set. We can rise to any level we wish. It is up to us—
specifically *us*—to improve our situation and to achieve success.

No one is going to hand us anything, but few are going to prevent us from gaining our proper share. More and more opportunities beckon. We must seize them—we must realize that today more than at any other time in history we have the means to go anywhere and do anything.

↜

When I first went into Hispanic marketing in the late '70s, I felt I was capitalizing on a *revolución* in North America. At conventions, meetings, seminars, on radio and television the same phrase was repeated: "The eighties will be the decade of the Hispanic—*la década del hispano*." The "ignored" Latino was suddenly discovered in every phase of society, from arts and education through women's issues. In 1978, *Time* magazine had made Latinos their cover story, discussing their new political and economic power, and it seemed to set off an awareness throughout the nation of a hitherto invisible segment of society. "What a nifty time to go to work," I thought. "I'm here at the peak—*en la papa*."

Well, it *was* a nifty time to work, but it was hardly the peak. Indeed, the '80s were a gentle rise compared to the Himalayas of the '90s. Now the *revolución* is in full force. Now it is time for Hispanics to understand their power and take advantage of it.

Truly, this is the peak time for Latinos in the United States. I wonder, though, what my children will say; they'll probably think the '90s were still the Dark Ages.

↜

Richard Bela, my friend for over fifteen years, runs a watchdog organization called the Hispanic Association on Corporate Responsibility (HACR), located in Washington, D.C. It has a simple mission statement: "The inclusion of Hispanics in the economic activities of corporate America in proportion to our economic activities." In other words, if Hispanics represent ten percent of the buying power in the U.S., they should get ten percent of the positions in American corporations.

Do they? Not yet. But Bela keeps up the pressure, and along

the way he has come up with the concept of three types of corporations: companies *que ya saben*—that "get it"; companies *que se estan despertando*—that are "waking up"; and companies *que siguen con los ojos cerrados*—that "don't get it." He has a number of criteria in each category, and I've refined them to make my own list, elements you should consider when—assuming you want to break into the corporate world—you look for a place to work.

Companies that "get it"

- Go to great lengths to understand their customers
- Get a high percentage of their sales—thus profits—from minority customers
- Tend to be publicly held
- Understand the value of maintaining good customer relations and achieving top-of-the-mind awareness among the public
- Have dealt in markets outside the U.S. and with other cultures worldwide for many years, and understand the differences
- Actively pursue good public relations, and try to avoid bad PR at all costs
- Demonstrate a care for their communities through philanthropy
- Value goodwill from minority constituencies
- Tend to hire the best young talent regardless of race or background

They include beverage companies, both beer and soft drinks; companies specializing in packaged goods; fast food companies; telecommunications companies (AT&T has thirteen Latino corporate vice presidents)—the companies, in other words, that sell to many markets and need them all for maximum profits.

Companies that are "waking up"

- Have recently realized the value of the ethnic consumer
- Have dealt in markets outside the U.S. and have an understanding of cultural differences
- Are actively cultivating a higher public profile

- May be publicly or privately held
- Have been socially or politically embarrassed by bad public relations regarding ethnic issues
- Have been boycotted by consumer groups or community groups for insensitivity to minorities

In this category the examples include airlines, banks and brokerage houses (Corestates Financial Corporation also has thirteen Hispanic vice presidents), electronics companies, health care companies, and petroleum refining companies. Until recently, these companies disregarded minority markets; now they have discovered the profits to be gained by actively reaching out to them (rather than assuming minorities will use their products, no matter what) and either because of outside pressure (bravo Bela!) or genuine goodwill have changed their awareness—are "waking up."

Companies that "don't get it"

- Have little or no reliance on the ethnic customer for sales or profitability (not that the ethnic customer doesn't patronize them—the customer simply has no other place to turn)
- Get their profits primarily by selling to middlemen, so have little or no direct contact with the end user, the customer
- Are usually but not necessarily privately held
- Feel no need to conform to pressure from "outsiders"
- Have little interest in their communities, since they feel that "communities" don't have a direct impact on sales or profitability
- Have few or no outreach programs into their communities or to the ethnic minorities in general
- Tend to hire people like themselves, and feel uncomfortable with those who are "different" from them

Utility companies, computer companies (IBM is a notable exception), apparel companies, and—yes—publishing companies are examples. My belief is that when minority buying power becomes even greater, these companies will change. They'll have to if they're not to go under.

Companies that "get it" are generally equally interested in long- and short-term profits; if there's an opportunity for sales, no matter how small as long as they'll increase profits, they'll go for it. In that sense, they're like first-rate politicians, who'll put aside prejudices to get votes; for them, votes *equal* profits. Look at South Carolina's Strom Thurmond, who's been in the Senate longer than any other man or woman. In the 1950s he was an outspoken segregationist; today he is vocal and active in support of civil rights. South Carolina has changed in forty years; the black voter has become increasingly important. Senator Thurmond might still be segregationist if his state hadn't changed. But change it did, and Thurmond was smart enough and wanted to keep his job badly enough to recognize it and change himself.

One hopes that companies are not catering to minority groups solely because of profits, or that even if profits are the initial motive, an awareness of equality and establishment of genuine partnerships will be the outgrowth. But I suspect that economics comes first, and that the companies that are "waking up" do so because they see increased profits in increased market share.

When a company realizes that future growth will come from the Hispanic market, it acts quickly, taking a number of practical steps:

1. It conducts research into the habits of the U.S. Latino population in many areas, including spending preferences, social conduct, family makeup, and attitudes toward relevant products.
2. It hires Hispanics as part of its staff to provide information on Latino groups and to interact with them.
3. It hires outside Hispanic consultants—advertisers, PR experts, marketers—to better reach the Latino markets.
4. It becomes active in the Latino community, doing both charitable and social work, contributing to the arts, education, and the like.
5. It conducts focus groups, asking for specific opinions about its products or services.

The Anglo managers I've talked to who have engaged in such programs speak passionately about their success—and about the unexpected side effect that seems common to them all. They've not only made profits from the Latino community, they've made friends—*¡amigos para la vida!* The natural discomfort existing between different cultural groups (particularly if the skin color is different) soon disappears. Common interests, common beliefs, common passions, even common jokes become the norm; similarities outweigh differences; mutual respect is born. More and more Anglos and Latinos *marry*. Hey, it's worked for Kathy and me.

~

The United States and Latin America are coming together. While it's too soon to project an American Union based on the model of the European Union, more and more we are becoming one continent, *una sola América,* 450,000,000 people (two-thirds Latino) with far more commonality than we perhaps realize. Inevitably, we will more and more depend on each other economically, educationally, and culturally (twenty years ago, the huge success in America of such writers as Allende and Márquez would have been unthinkable).

Thus today and increasingly into the future, Latinos have an important role to play in American corporations, particularly the "get-it's" and "waking-up's." That role, while ultimately leading to increased corporate profits, is initially one of forming cultural and business bonds. Far more than most Anglos, we can move comfortably between the Anglo and Latino worlds, feel no strangeness with customs Anglos *see* as strange (including getting through "customs" at the airport!), and are able to talk to our brothers and sisters as equals, neither condescending nor diffident. After all, *somos familia*—we're family. We know that what's good for one country is good for another, that "fairness" presupposes respect. Just because the CEO of a Latin American company chooses not to speak English doesn't mean he isn't every bit as shrewd as or even shrewder than his Anglo counterpart. I believe that because of the geographical situation, our educational opportunities, and our increased desire for personal success, U.S. Latinos are *the* bridge between the Americas. Corporations would be crazy not to want us—and most of them know it. They need us. *¡Nos necesitan!*

And as Latinos become more prominent in corporations, they'll work to make those corporations do more business with Hispanic suppliers. Not because the corporation feels a responsibility to engage minority-owned firms, but because those firms, just like the Latino executives, know what the Latino market wants and can help the corporations reach it.

I'm struck by the young Latino businessperson of today. He or she is able to live in this cross-cultural world with an ease that I as a young man would never have thought possible. Richard Bela describes such young *profesionales* as *looking* like Anglos (business suits, designer briefcases, all the "dress for success" stuff, indistinguishable from their Anglo counterparts except perhaps for the deeper color of their skin). They even *act* a bit more like Anglos (they do their aerobics, play golf, frequent the "in" restaurants and bars outside the barrio). But on the whole their values remain quite different from an Anglo's. They still put family first, still make room in their lives for activities other than business, are more religious and more community oriented. Perhaps because their own parents spent so much time guiding them, they will set aside time for their own children.

Of course, as corporations globalize, their top managers become more aware of, and open to, cultural differences. They recognize that the time of the almighty U.S. company has passed, and are adopting the win-win strategy of being equals with other countries *con respeto* to other methods of doing business. Their lower-echelon executives, no matter how young, have probably already traveled abroad—I know a thirty-year-old Anglo corporate lawyer who has already been to Europe eleven times and to Japan seven. But most of the interaction has been East-West, not North-South. The field in that direction is still vast and needs employees who can "talk Latin-American."

So educated ethnic kids are valuable. They bring everything to the table a young Anglo brings, *plus* a knowledge of Spanish. And because they're young, they're cheap. Therefore the opportunities are far greater at an entry level than they are higher up on the management ladder. Middle-aged middle managers are naturally protective of their positions and will fight *anyone*, Latinos included, who seem likely to replace them. Richard Bela has found that resistance and discrimination are still prevalent at the directors' level. In time, of course, as the directors retire and new, more culturally oriented managers take their place, the discrimination will fade.

⌒

Even as corporations begin to recognize the need to cultivate the minority communities, the communities have begun to recognize their own power over corporations. When Denny's was found to discriminate against black employees, the public outcry (and tacit boycott) forced them to change their policy. When Texaco executives were secretly recorded making racially disparaging remarks, Peter Bijur, the CEO, took quick action: He apologized, publicly faced the problem head-on, and negotiated a multi-million-dollar settlement. Now Texaco is communicating its involvement in the Hispanic community as well as the African-American community, to the benefit of all. If ten percent of the population stays away from a product, its producer will listen. If twenty percent (Latinos *and* African-Americans) don't buy, the company will change its management until discrimination is eliminated. *El dinero habla*— money talks.

But it's my hope that protest and boycotts will become less and less needed. When companies hire Hispanics, and when the entry-level employees reach higher positions within the companies, discrimination will decrease. Enlightened corporations know this. Anheuser Busch, American Bankers Insurance, Diamond Shamrock Incorporated (a petroleum refining company), and Dow Chemical, among others, already have two or more Hispanics on their boards of directors. It's impossible to think they will ever revert to a time when the minority community is overlooked.

And the more a corporation interacts with the Hispanic community, the more mutuality of interest develops. Anheuser Busch, Coca-Cola, Ford, PepsiCo, Phillip Morris, AT&T, Chrysler, Coors, McDonald's and RJR Nabisco are the top-ranked corporations when it comes to corporate philanthropy in the Hispanic community. All of them are *Latino* household names as well as Anglo ones.

‿

The above are the external positive factors that mean better careers and more opportunity for Hispanic-Americans. In sum, "they're" making it easier for us because they need us. And we can make it easier for ourselves by recognizing the *internal* factors. Any obstacle can be overcome if we know what it looks like and how it bars our way. By understanding the concepts in *The Americano Dream,* middle-aged businesspeople and entrepreneurs can surely improve their chances for success. Young businesspersons can shape their careers to the model I've described in the preceding chapters.

And finally, there are the young people—the kids and the teenagers. They are our hopes, and it is to them we must give our fullest commitment and attention. We need to do more for them. We need to do it early. We need to do it *now.*

We must keep these imperatives constantly in mind:

- *Really* teach our children where we come from—our culture, our inheritance—through our communities, through our schools, but mostly one-on-one, parent to child.
- Impress pride on our children and teach them that they're like everybody else—never "inferior," never "second class," never "other."
- Teach them that race doesn't matter. It's not "us against them, them against us." Teach them that their pride in being Latino is equal to their friend's pride in being African-American. Don't scapegoat. Teach them inner confidence and universal love.
- Plant the idea early of going to college. Fill their heads with the images of success an education can bring, and praise them for their academic achievements. Let them overhear us telling friends and family: "Sara's really smart. She's going to wind up at a good university." It's amazing how often our kids will fulfill our expectations. So expect greatness. Expect joy.

- Spend lots of time with them, particularly from their birth to age eighteen, after that *they'll* want to spend time with you. *They'll* seek you out. Read to them. Play with them. Learn with them. Make it fun. We'll all benefit if we concentrate on their troubles and not our own. The human brain grows as the body grows. If it is not stimulated—exercised—it will not develop as it can.
- Help with their homework. Go with them to their classes, their clubs, their sporting events. Get to know their teachers, their friends, and their friends' parents. Discuss their mutual problems, and celebrate when the problems are overcome.
- Get serious with them during the high school years. This is where good grades matter. They'll fight for their "space," for time to date, for independence. But they'll need to study, and if you've been close in the earlier years, they'll listen and they'll compromise.
- Keep your advice positive and fair. Kids will slack off from time to time, testing your boundaries. So set up expectations for them, and make sure the message is positive if they do not always meet them. "Mostly As and Bs? Well done! Now what can we do about that C?" is far better than "What—a C? You know you can do better than that!"
- Help them with their college applications. Encourage. Encourage. Encourage.
- Give them roots and wings. There's a time to let go. Overcome the Latino cultural trait of wanting to keep the children home or at least bring them back. Let them fly. It's their sky.

Do the figures cited at the beginning of this chapter make me pessimistic? Not at all! My own life and the increasing number of Latino success stories convince me that it is only a matter of a very short time—and one or two very short steps—before the figures turn around. The Americano dream? It exists, it is realistic, and it is there for all of us to share.

INDEX

Lionel Sosa is the embodiment of the Americano dream. One of the most successful Latino entrepreneurs in this country, he worked his way up from the poverty-stricken west side of San Antonio, Texas, to become a high-profile advertising executive in the upper echelons of the American business world. Sosa overcame what he calls the "Hispanic mind-set of underachievement," and his impressive career—based on initiative and perseverance, ambition, and *huevos*—is an inspiration to other Latinos eager to take their places in the Anglo business world of overachievement.

The *Americano Dream* tells you everything you need to know to become a successful entrepreneur. Drawing on his own marketing expertise and decades of invaluable business experience, Sosa offers practical, hard-hitting advice to other Latinos who aspire to success in business and in life. With honesty and insight, he explains how Latino cultural views can become barriers to success and describes how to develop clear goals and strategies, effective approaches to problem-solving, and most important of all, an assertive, can-do attitude. Sosa also tells you how to master the arts of planning, communication, and negotiation, as well as providing guidance on ways to increase self-confidence and transform your cultural heritage into an asset that can become a viable tool for success.

Including illuminating anecdotes from the lives of other high-profile Hispanics such as Edward James Olmos, Henry Cisneros, Gloria Estefan, Coca-Cola CEO Roberto Goizueta, and Geraldo Rivera, *The Americano Dream* also profiles what Sosa calls eight Hispanic business stereotypes and describes the twelve essential traits of successful Latino entrepreneurs.

In an increasingly multicultural nation where ethnic markets have become valuable prizes, Lionel Sosa proves that it isn't impossible to hold on to your heritage and to be successful, too. The only book of its kind, *The Americano Dream* is a groundbreaking, empowering guide to achievement that is destined to become the bible for all Latinos who want to compete—and win—in American business and society.

LIONEL SOSA is currently CEO of KJS, a multi-cultural advertising agency that helps Fortune 500 companies expand their businesses into the Latino, Asian, and African-American markets. He was the founder of the largest Hispanic ad agency in the United States, Sosa, Bromley, Aguilar, Noble & Associates (now Bromley Aguilar), and was later Chairman of DMB&B Americas, a network of 20 ad agencies specializing in Latin America. He has been featured on the *Today* show, on the cover of *Fortune*, and in the *Wall Street Journal*, the *New York Times*, *U.S. News and World Report*, *Forbes*, the *Dallas Times Herald*, and in the September 1996 issue of *Texas Monthly*, where he was named one of the "most impressive, intriguing, and influential Texans of 1996."